THE
LITTLE BOOK
OF
IKIGAI

THE
LITTLE BOOK
OF
IKIGAI

THE ESSENTIAL JAPANESE
WAY TO FINDING YOUR
PURPOSE IN LIFE

●

KEN MOGI

Quercus

First published in Great Britain in 2017 by

Quercus Editions Ltd
Carmelite House
50 Victoria Embankment
London EC4Y 0DZ

An Hachette UK company

A CIP catalogue record for this book is available
from the British Library

ISBN 978 1 78648 903 6

Illustrations by Amber Anderson

10 9 8 7 6 5 4 3 2 1

Text designed and typeset by CC Book Production
Printed and bound in Great Britain by Clays Ltd, St Ives plc

Contents

Note to the Reader: The Five Pillars of *ikigai*   vii

Chapter 1: What is *ikigai*?   1

Chapter 2: Your reason to get up in the morning   19

Chapter 3: *Kodawari* and the benefits of thinking small   35

Chapter 4: The sensory beauty of *ikigai*   59

Chapter 5: Flow and creativity   75

Chapter 6: *Ikigai* and sustainability   99

Chapter 7: Finding your purpose in life   119

Chapter 8: What doesn't kill you makes you stronger   143

Chapter 9: *Ikigai* and happiness   161

Chapter 10: Accept yourself for who you are   179

Conclusion: Find your own *ikigai*   191

The Five Pillars of *ikigai*

Throughout this book, I refer to the Five Pillars of *ikigai*. They are:

Pillar 1:   Starting small

Pillar 2:   Releasing yourself

Pillar 3:   Harmony and sustainability

Pillar 4:   The joy of little things

Pillar 5:   Being in the here and now

These pillars come up frequently, because each one provides the supportive framework – the very foundations – that allows *ikigai* to flourish. They are not mutually exclusive or exhaustive, nor do they have a particular order or hierarchy. But they are vital to our understanding of *ikigai*, and will provide guidance as you digest what you read in the forth-coming pages and reflect on your own life. Each time they will come back to you with a renewed and deepened sense of significance.

I hope you enjoy this journey of exploration.

THE
LITTLE BOOK
OF
IKIGAI

CHAPTER 1

What is *ikigai*?

When President Barack Obama made his official visit to Japan in the spring of 2014, it befell Japanese government officials to choose a venue for the welcome dinner to be hosted by the Prime Minister of Japan. The occasion was to be a private affair, preceding the state visit which was due to start officially the following day, and which included a ceremonial dinner at the Imperial Palace, with the Emperor and Empress presiding.

Imagine how much consideration went into the choice of restaurant. When it was finally announced that the venue was to be Sukiyabashi Jiro, arguably one of the world's most famous and respected sushi restaurants, the decision was met with universal approval. Indeed, you could tell how much President Obama himself enjoyed the experience of dining there from the smile on his face when he stepped out. Reportedly, Obama said it was the best sushi he had ever eaten. That was a huge compliment coming from someone who grew up in Hawaii, with exposure to a strong Japanese influence including sushi, and who, presumably, had had many previous experiences of *haute cuisine*.

Sukiyabashi Jiro is proudly headed by Jiro Ono, who is, as I write this, the world's oldest living three-Michelin-star chef, at the age of ninety-one. Sukiyabashi Jiro was already famous among Japanese connoisseurs before the first Michelin Guide for Tokyo in 2012, but that publication definitely put the restaurant on the world gourmet map.

Although the sushi he produces is shrouded in an almost mystic aura, Ono's cooking is based on practical and resourceful techniques. For example, he developed a special procedure for providing salmon roe (*ikura*) in a fresh condition throughout the year. This challenged the long-held professional wisdom followed in the best sushi restaurants – that *ikura* should only be served during its prime season, the autumn, when the salmon brave the rivers to lay their eggs. He also invented a special procedure in which a certain type of fish meat is smoked with burned rice straw to produce a special flavour. The timing of the placing of the sushi plates in front of eagerly waiting guests must be precisely calculated, as must the temperature of the fish meat, in order to optimize the sushi's taste.(It is assumed that the customer will put the food in his mouth without too much delay.) In fact, dining at Sukiyabashi Jiro is like experiencing an exquisite ballet, choreographed from behind the counter by a dignified and respected master with an austere demeanour (although his face will, by the way, crack into a smile from time to time, if you are lucky).

You can take it that Ono's incredible success is due to exceptional talent, sheer determination and bloody-minded perseverance over years of hard work, as well as a relentless pursuit of culinary techniques and presentation of the highest quality. Needless to say, Ono has achieved all of this.

However, more than that and perhaps above all else, Ono has *ikigai*. It is no exaggeration to say that he owes his incredibly fabulous success in the professional and private realms of his life to the refinement of this most Japanese ethos.

Ikigai is a Japanese word for describing the pleasures and meanings of life. The word literally consists of '*iki*' (to live) and '*gai*' (reason).

In the Japanese language, *ikigai* is used in various contexts, and can apply to small everyday things as well as to big goals and achievements. It is such a common word that people use it in daily life quite casually, without being aware of its having any special significance. Most importantly, *ikigai* is possible without your necessarily being successful in your professional life. In this sense, it is a very democratic concept, steeped in a celebration of the diversity of life. It is true that having *ikigai* can result in success, but success is not a requisite condition for having *ikigai*. It is open to every one of us.

For an owner of a successful sushi restaurant such as Jiro Ono, being offered a compliment from the President of the United States is a source of *ikigai*. To be recognized as the world's oldest Michelin three-star chef certainly counts as a rather nice piece of *ikigai*. However, *ikigai* is not limited to these domains of worldly recognition and acclaim. Ono might find *ikigai* simply in serving the best tuna to a smiling customer or in feeling the refreshing chill of the early morning air, as he gets up and prepares to go to the

Tsukiji fish market. Ono might even find *ikigai* in the cup of coffee he sips before starting each day. Or in a ray of sunshine coming through the leaves of a tree as he walks to his restaurant in central Tokyo.

Ono once mentioned that he wishes to die while making sushi. It clearly gives him a deep sense of *ikigai*, despite the fact that it requires many small steps that are in themselves monotonous and time-consuming. In order to make the octopus meat soft and tasty, for example, Ono has to 'massage' the cephalopod mollusc for one hour. Preparing Kohada, a small shiny fish considered to be the king of sushi, also needs much attention, involving the removal of the fish's scales and intestines, and a precisely balanced marinade using salt and vinegar. 'Perhaps my last sushi making would be Kohada', he said.

Ikigai resides in the realm of small things. The morning air, the cup of coffee, the ray of sunshine, the massaging of octopus meat and the American President's praise are on an equal footing. Only those who can recognize the richness of this whole spectrum really appreciate and enjoy it.

This is an important lesson of *ikigai*. In a world where our value as people and our own sense of self-worth is determined primarily by our success, many people are under unnecessary pressure. You might feel that any value system you have is only worthy and justified if it translates into concrete achievements – a promotion, for example, or a lucrative investment.

Well, relax! You can have *ikigai*, a value to live by, without necessarily having to prove yourself in that way. That is not to say that it will come easily. I sometimes have to remind myself of this truth, even though I was born and grew up in a country where *ikigai* is more or less an assumed knowledge.

In a TED talk titled 'How to live to be 100+', American writer Dan Buettner discussed *ikigai* specifically as an ethos for good health and longevity. At the time of writing, Buettner's talk has been viewed more than three million times. Buettner explains the traits of the life styles of five places in the world where people live longer. Each 'blue zone', as Buettner terms these areas, has its own culture and traditions that contribute to longevity. The zones are Okinawa in Japan; Sardinia in Italy; Nicoya in Costa Rica; Icaria in Greece; and among the Seventh-day Adventists in Loma

Linda, California. Of all these blue zones, the Okinawans enjoy the highest life expectancy.

Okinawa is a chain of islands in the southern-most part of the Japanese archipelago. It boasts a lot of centenarians. Buettner cites the words of its inhabitants as testimonies of what constitute *ikigai*: a 102-year-old Karate master told him that his *ikigai* was caring for his martial arts; a hundred-year-old fisherman said his could be found by continuing to catch fish for his family three times a week; a 102-year-woman said hers was in holding her tiny great-great-great-grand-daughter – she said it was like leaping into heaven. Woven together, these simple lifestyle choices give clues as to what constitutes the very essence of *ikigai*: a sense of community, a balanced diet and an awareness of spirituality.

Although perhaps more obvious in Okinawa, these principles are shared by people in Japan in general. After all, the longevity rate in Japan is extremely high everywhere in the country. According to a 2016 survey by the Ministry of Health, Labour and Welfare, compared to other countries and regions in the world, Japanese men's longevity ranked fourth in the world, with an average life expectancy of 80.79

years, after Hong Kong, Iceland and Switzerland. Japanese women lived the second longest in the world, with an average life expectancy of 87.05 years, after Hong Kong and followed by Spain.

It is fascinating to see the extent to which *ikigai* comes naturally to many Japanese. A key study concerning the health benefits of *ikigai* published in 2008 (*Sense of Life Worth Living (ikigai) and Mortality in Japan: Ohsaki Study*, Sone et al. 2008) was conducted by researchers at the Tohoku University medical school based in Sendai city in northern Japan. This study involved a large number of subjects, enabling the researchers to derive statistically significant correlations between *ikigai* and various health benefits.

In this study, the researchers analysed data from the Ōsaki National Health Insurance (NHI) cohort study, conducted over a period of seven years. A self-administered questionnaire was distributed to 54,996 beneficiaries of The Ōsaki Public Health Centre, a local government agency that provides health services to the residents of fourteen municipalities, aged between forty and seventy-nine years.

The survey consisted of a ninety-three-item questionnaire

in which the subjects were asked about past medical and family histories, physical health status, drinking and smoking habits, job, marital status, education and other health-related factors, including *ikigai*. The crucial question relating to the latter was very direct: 'Do you have *ikigai* in your life?' The subjects were asked to choose one of three answers: 'yes', 'uncertain' or 'no'.

Analysing data from more than 50,000 people, the Ōsaki study paper concluded that 'as compared with those who found a sense of *ikigai*, those who did not were more likely to be unmarried, unemployed, have a lower educational level, have bad or poor self-rated health, have a high level of perceived mental stress, have severe or moderate bodily pain, have limitation of physical function and be less likely to walk'.

Using just this study, it is of course not possible to tell whether having *ikigai* has led to improved marital, employment or educational status of the subjects, or, alternatively, whether the accumulation of the various small successes in life has led to an increased sense of *ikigai*. But it would be reasonably safe to say that having a sense of *ikigai* points to a frame of mind whereby the subjects feel that they can build a happy and active life. *Ikigai* is, in a sense, a barometer which reflects a person's outlook on life in an integrated and representative way.

Furthermore, the mortality rate for people who answered 'yes' to the *ikigai* question was significantly lower than for those who answered 'no'. The lower rate was the result of their being at a lower risk of cardiovascular disease. Interestingly, there was no significant change in the risk of cancer for people who answered 'yes' compared to those who answered 'no' to the *ikigai* question.

Why did the people with *ikigai* also have a reduced risk of suffering from cardiovascular disease? Maintenance of good health involves a large number of factors. It is difficult to say definitely what factors are ultimately responsible but the reduction of cardiovascular disease would suggest that those who have *ikigai* are more likely to exercise, since engagement in physical activities is known to reduce the risk of cardio-vascular disease. Indeed, the Ōsaki study found that those who answered positively about *ikigai* did exercise more than those who gave a negative response.

Ikigai gives your life a purpose, while giving you the grit to carry on. Although Sukiyabashi Jiro is now a world-famous culinary destination frequented by people such as Joël Robuchon, Jiro Ono's origins are very humble. His family struggled to make ends meet and out of financial necessity (these were the days before the introduction of regulations banning child labour in Japan), he started to work in a restaurant in the evenings when he was just an elementary school boy. During the day at school, tired from working long and arduous hours, he tended to nod off in class. When the teacher made him stand outside as punishment, he would often take advantage of the break from lessons to run back to the restaurant and finish chores, or to get a head start and reduce his workload.

When Ono started his first sushi restaurant, the one that would eventually lead to Sukiyabashi Jiro, his aspiration was not to create the world's finest dining establishment. At that time, it was simply cheaper to open a sushi restaurant, compared to other types of restaurant. Sushi restaurants, in their basic form, require only the most rudimentary equipment and furnishings. This is unsurprising, when you consider that sushi started as street food sold from stalls in the Edo period in the seventeenth century. For Ono at that time, opening a sushi restaurant was an effort to make ends meet, nothing more, nothing less.

Then started the long and arduous climb upwards. However, at every stage of his long career, Ono had *ikigai* to help support and motivate him as he listened to his own inner voice in his relentless pursuit of quality. This was not something that could be mass marketed, or easily understood by the general public. Ono had to pat himself on the shoulder along the way, especially in the early days when society at large had yet to take any notice of his strenuous efforts.

He quietly got on with making small improvements to his business, designing a special container, for example, that fitted within the unusual counter space of his restaurant, so as to make everything neat and clean. He improved several tools used in the preparation of sushi, unaware that many of them would go on to be used in other restaurants and would eventually be recognized as being his original invention. All these small advancements have been labours of love, supported by Ono's keen sense of the significance of **starting small** (the first pillar of *ikigai*).

*

This little book wishes to be a humble help for those who are interested in the ethos of *ikigai*. I hope that by telling Jiro Ono's story I have given a flavour of what this concept entails and how valuable it can be. As we will see together, having *ikigai* can literally transform your life. You can live longer, have good health, become happier, more satisfied, and less stressed. In addition, and as a by-product of *ikigai*, you may even become more creative and successful. You can have all these benefits of *ikigai*, if you know how to appreciate this philosophy of life and learn to apply it in your life.

Because *ikigai* is a concept heavily immersed in Japanese culture and its heritage, in order to clarify what it entails, I will be delving deep into Japan's traditions, while seeking relevance in its contemporary mores. In my view, *ikigai* is a kind of cognitive and behavioural hub, around which various life habits and value systems are organized. The fact the Japanese have been using *ikigai* in their everyday lives, not always necessarily knowing what the term means exactly, is a testimony of the importance of *ikigai,* especially if you take into account the lexical hypothesis, first put forward by the English psychologist Francis Galton in the late nineteenth century. According to Galton, important individual traits in a race's personality become encoded in the language of the culture, and the more important the trait, the more likely it is to be captured in a single word. The fact that *ikigai* has been formed as a single denomination means that the concept points to a major psychological characteristic relevant to the life of the Japanese. *Ikigai* represents the Japanese wisdom of life, the sensitivities and manners of action that have been uniquely pertinent in Japanese society, and that have evolved over hundreds of years within the closely knit society of the island nation.

I will show you that of course you don't have to be Japanese to have *ikigai*. When I think of *ikigai* as a private pleasure, I remember a special chair I encountered in the United Kingdom.

For a couple of years in the middle of the 1990s, I was doing postdoctoral research in the Physiological Laboratory at the University of Cambridge. I was lodging in a house owned by an eminent professor. When he showed me the room I would be staying in, he pointed to a chair and explained that it had sentimental value for him: his father had made it especially for him when he was a small child.

There was nothing extraordinary about the chair. To be honest, it was rather clumsily made. The design was not refined, and there were ragged, irregular features here and there. If the chair was for sale in a market, it wouldn't have fetched much money. Having said that, I could also see, by the glimmer in the professor's eyes, that the chair had a very special meaning for him. And that was all that mattered. It had a unique place in the professor's heart, just because his father had made it for him. That is what sentimental values are all about.

This is just a small example, but it is a powerful one. *Ikigai* is like the professor's chair. It is about discovering, defining and appreciating those of life's pleasures that have meaning for you. It is OK if no one else sees that particular value, although as we have seen with Ono and as you will find throughout this book, pursuing one's private joys in life often leads to social rewards. You can find and cultivate your own *ikigai*, grow it secretly and slowly, until one day it bears a quite original fruit.

Throughout this book, while reviewing ways of living, culture, tradition, mindsets and philosophy of life in Japan, we will discover suggestions for good health and longevity that are entrenched within *ikigai* and you can ask yourself along the way:

- What are your most sentimental values?
- What are the small things that give you pleasure?

These are good places to start when it comes to finding your own *ikigai* as a way to a happier, more fulfilled life.

CHAPTER 2

Your reason to get up in the morning

For some people, getting out of bed is not a problem. For others, it seems very hard to do. If you are one of those people who lingers under the duvet after the alarm clock goes off, wishing that it was a holiday, only able to drag yourself out of bed reluctantly after the second or third wake-up call, then this chapter is for you.

Ikigai is sometimes expressed as 'the reason for getting up in the morning'. It is what gives you an ongoing motivation for living your life, or you could also say that it gives you the appetite for life that makes you eager to greet each new day. As we will see in this chapter, the Japanese do not need grandiose motivational frameworks to keep going, but rely more on the little rituals in their daily routines. Of the Five Pillars of *ikigai* described at the beginning of this book, getting up early has the most to do with **starting small**.

Hiroki Fujita, who trades in tuna in Tokyo's famous Tsukiji fish market, is no stranger to the ethos of getting up early in the morning. He gets up at 2.00 am, and prepares to go to work, following his usual protocols. It is still dark when he arrives at his shop in the market, even in the middle of summer. Fujita immediately starts to work in the same brisk manner he's been accustomed to for so many years.

There is a special reason why Fujita gets up that early every day. As a broker for tuna fish, he needs to get hold of the finest tuna, and therefore can't afford to miss anything important that goes on at the market. Fujita's customers depend on him. As the world discovers the heavenly, delectable taste of *toro* tuna, more and more attention is given to the process of selecting and seasoning the best specimens. Fujita examines dozens of tuna laid out on the floor of a special section of the Tsukiji fish market, trying to choose the best one for his impressive list of clients, most of them the top sushi restaurants in and around Tokyo, including, of course, Sukiyabashi Jiro.

Choosing a good tuna is an intricate art in itself, says Fujita. At Tsukiji, tuna fish are sold whole, and the tuna broker cannot see the inside of the fish when making a purchase. The only means by which a tuna broker can select the fish in the market is by looking at the surface of the meat near the caudal fin which has been chopped off the body of the fish. Fujita often touches and feels the fish at the caudal fin cut, using his fingers to tell if the meat inside is mature.

'The public can have misconceptions about what kind of tuna is tasty', says Fujita:

People tend to think that red, fresh-looking tuna is best, but nothing could be further from the truth. The best tuna actually has a more subdued appearance. That comes only with a certain kind of fish body, captured by a limited range of fishing procedures. The best kind can be found only in, say, one out of a hundred. One tries to find certain looks and textures, but it is difficult to be sure, as the best ones are often very similar to, if not indistinguishable from, those damaged through oxidation. I get up early in the morning, because I am always in pursuit of that special kind of fish. I think to myself, would I find the one, if I go to the fish market today? That thought keeps me going.

We should, perhaps, all be embracing the morning the way Fujita does. We know enough about the physiological conditions of the brain to know that that time of day is best for productive and creative work. Data suggests that during sleep, the brain is busy registering memories within its neural circuits as the day's activities are sorted and consolidated. There is still ongoing research as to the dynamics of memory consolidation. It would appear that new memories are temporarily stored in the brain with the help of the region known as the hippocampus (we are sure of this essential role of the hippocampus, as people with substantial damages to it are no longer able to form new memories). Then those memories appear gradually to 'migrate' into the associate cortex to be consolidated into long-term memories. The brain is able to do all this efficient storing, linking and indexing of memories in the absence of incoming sensory information.

In the morning, assuming you have had a sufficient amount

24

of sleep, the brain has finished its important night job. It is in a refreshed state, ready to absorb new information as you start a day's activities. Saying good morning – *ohayo* in Japanese – and making eye contact activates the brain's reward systems and leads to a better functioning of its hormonal regulation, which results in an improved immune system. All these effects have been shown to be statistically significant, although the causal links are not completely understood. As we will see below, the ethos of getting up early in the morning is embedded in Japanese culture, so it comes as no surprise, perhaps, that there are rules about how and when to say *ohayo*. These things are taken seriously! As various hormonal regulations in the brain are known to be in harmony with the processions of the sun, it therefore makes sense to live in synchrony with the sun, as the circadian rhythms are tuned to the natural cycles of day and night.

That is the neurological explanation for why getting up so early is so much a part of Japanese tradition. But, as we were just saying, there is also a cultural one: Japan is a nation which has always placed a high value on the morning sun.

Prince Shōtoku, who ruled Japan in the seventh century

and was a son of Emperor Yōmei, was a man of prodigious talents. According to legend, he could listen to and comprehend ten people speaking at the same time. Prince Shōtoku is credited for introducing affirmative political reforms, such as a seventeen-article constitution, which famously stressed the importance of *wa* (harmony) in its very first article (of which more later).

When sending an official letter to the Emperor of China, Prince Shōtoku began with the sentence, 'From the sovereign of the land of the rising sun.' This was a reference to the fact that Japan is situated east of China, the direction in which the sun rises. The image somehow stuck, and Japan is still sometimes regarded as 'the land of the rising sun' in Western civilization. *Japan* is an exonym; in the Japanese language the name of the nation is Nippon or Nihon, two alternative pronunciations for the nomenclature expressing 'the origin of the sun'. The national flag of Japan, *hinomaru* ('circle of the sun') is a visualization of the idea of the land of the rising sun.

The sun has been the object of worship, as something that symbolizes life and energy, for a long time in Japan. On New Year's Day, many people get up early (or stay awake all night) to see the first rising sun of the year. It is customary to climb Mt Fuji in the night, so as to revere the rising sun from the peak. Many Japanese brands, including beer, newspaper, life insurance, matches and a television station use the rising sun as their theme.

Another reason why the Japanese like to get an early start goes back to the economic history of the country. During the Edo era (1603–1868) when Japan was ruled by the Tokugawa Shogunate, approximately 80% of the whole population were farmers. Even after the rapid industrialization and urbanization, about 50% of Japanese were still farmers in 1945. And for the sake of successful farming, it is necessary to get up early in the morning.

That farming has had such an impact is perhaps no surprise, given how reliant on rice the Japanese economy has been. Rice was the most important, almost sacred product of the land. It had to be offered to gods in rituals, and the rice cake symbolized the coming of the New Year. *Sake*, the popular Japanese alcoholic drink, is made from rice. Sacred decorations at Shinto shrines are made from rice straws.

Today, the percentage of people engaged in agriculture has

dropped to 1.5 of the whole population. The relative importance of farming in the mindset of the average Japanese has diminished. However, many conceptual frameworks related to farming are still alive today, influencing people's attitudes in daily life. For example, the planting of rice sprouts in the spring and harvesting in the autumn is one of the most important rituals conducted by the Emperor. The specially designated rice fields are in the Imperial Palace grounds in Tokyo. Both the planting and harvesting is done by his Imperial Majesty's own hand, and the scene is broadcast on national television. In his role as representative of the Japanese people, the Emperor does this because this was something the majority of the population did for a living.

It was not only farmers who had the ethos of getting up early in the morning. Among merchants, it was traditionally considered commendable to get up at dawn and start the day's work straight away, in order to get ahead with business, but also to save fuel and candles during the night. There is an old Japanese proverb, 'getting up early is a profit of three *mon*', the *mon* being the currency of Japan during the Muromachi period (1336–1870). The saying is roughly equivalent to the English proverb 'the early bird catches the worm'. There is a general perception among the Japanese populace that getting up early makes economic sense. And today we see this whether it's tuna merchants getting up in the night to go to the market or workaholic businesspersons in the financial sector going to the office in the early hours to respond to activities in foreign markets.

One perhaps unlikely profession which takes the 'before breakfast' ethos literally in contemporary Japan is the sumo one. Sumo wrestlers famously train in the morning, before they have breakfast. Actually, sumo training is done *only* in the morning. In the afternoon, the wrestlers take it easy, having a nap, or immersing themselves in their favourite hobbies. Needless to say, the nap and playtime come only after a generous helping of food, which helps the wrestlers build their famous oversized bodies.

Radio taiso (radio calisthenics – short exercises set to music) is perhaps more representative of Japan's morning-oriented culture of physical activity. And this one is for ordinary people of all ages.

Conceived in 1928 by the government to improve the

physical fitness of the general public, *radio taiso* has been a regular custom (except for a break of four years after the Second World War) among the Japanese ever since. Many are introduced to it at primary school. Children in their first year of education are taught how to move their arms and legs in synchronization with the music, as the actions are simple enough for six-year-olds to imitate. During the summer holidays, local meetings of *radio taiso* are held, which children are encouraged to attend with rewards of collectable stamps. If a child accumulates a certain number of stamps on a stamp card, they are given a present such as sweets or stationery at the end of the holiday. This custom is supposed to have great educational value, in encouraging children to go to sleep early and wake up in the morning, a healthy habit to establish especially in an era where digital entertainments such as games and YouTube videos tend to keep them awake late into the night. Children are therefore encouraged to carry the spirit of the 'rising sun', although not in a nationalistic way. *Radio taiso* is an example of a small dose of ingenuity going a very long distance.

Radio taiso is sometimes practised at construction sites

and factories, where physical preparation for work is deemed necessary, and, even in white collar offices, before a day's work begins.

Nowadays, it is mainly senior people who duly practice *radio taiso*. It is not uncommon to see a group of elders gathered at a park in residential areas for the daily morning exercise. They take their positions at precisely 6.30 am, just as NHK Radio 1 starts broadcasting the theme music of *radio taiso*. It is their *ikigai*.

The image of people in uniform exercising in unison has sometimes been used by the international media to portray the image of Japan as a group-oriented country. At the early morning *radio taiso* gatherings of the elderly, the movements are not at all orderly or synchronized. You find people scattered all over the place, each with their own individualistic approach to the calisthenics. Some are out of step with the music, while others are chatting briskly while moving their arms and legs. Some just join in the middle of music, while others might leave before the end. In other words, there is an abundance of idiosyncrasies, and they are tolerated.

Radio taiso is perhaps an apotheosis of the Japanese ethos of prizing early morning activities. It is particularly interesting from the point of view of the social building of *ikigai*, because it brings together a community, in keeping with **harmony and sustainability**, the third pillar. It has had other repercussions too. The music for *radio taiso* has come to occupy among the Japanese people a special position and has been featured in many Japanese popular films and dramas.

The joy of little things seems particularly pertinent in this context, given that it is customary in Japan to have something sweet first thing in the morning, traditionally with green tea, although increasingly this has been replaced with coffee or black tea. It certainly makes sense. No matter where you are in the world, if you make a habit of having your favourite things soon after you get up (for example, chocolate and coffee), dopamine will be released in your brain, reinforcing the actions (getting up) prior to the receipt of your reward (chocolate and coffee). As Mary Poppins famously sang in the eponymous musical, 'a spoonful of sugar helps the medicine go down'.

Other small things can help you get out of bed in the morning. Many Japanese have a long commute, especially in and around metropolitan areas such as Tokyo, Nagoya, and Osaka. I myself used to take a 6.20 am train to go to my senior high school. I would sit in the same carriage every time. There were always some familiar faces in the seats nearby. What was remarkable, and cheering, was that every morning several office workers would be playing *shogi* (Japanese chess) together, enjoying themselves on their commute. This *shogi* club was something like the *radio taiso* club, using the power of community to enhance the motivation for an early commute (the third pillar of *ikigai*, **harmony and sustainability**). To this day, I remember the sight as something close to the image of perfect happiness.

Thus, *radio taiso* and *shogi* can be a regarded as a well-devised scheme for promoting the first, third and fourth pillars of *ikigai*, namely **starting small, harmony and sustainability**, and **the joy of little things**.

Needless to say, you don't have to be born in Japan to practise the custom of getting up early. After all, every land is a land of the rising sun. Seen from the space station, there is no difference. At any moment, the sun is rising for some locations, and setting for others.

Perhaps you could try your own version of *radio taiso*, or *shogi* club, immersed in your own local culture. You might want to start a book club with the regular commuters on your journey, or prepare a delicious breakfast that you can look forward to after a gentle jog or stretching exercises. Make **the joy of little things** work for you, then you can also start your *ikigai* in the morning.

CHAPTER 3

Kodawari and the benefits of thinking small

In recent years, Japan has become a popular tourist destination. In the year 2010, nearly 8 million people from abroad visited the country. In the year 2015, the figure increased to nearly 20 million. It has become common to see hordes of tourists walking the streets of such popular destinations as Tokyo, Kyoto, and Osaka. Tourists can also now be spotted in remote villages, in restaurants hitherto known only to locals, as they brave places that traditionally were avoided.

Ever since the modernization of the nation, the Japanese government has been trying to lure foreign tourists. In the Meiji era (1868–1912), a number of western style hotels were built, welcoming tourists from Europe and the United States. In those times, Japan was not an industrialized exporting economy, so the foreign currency those tourists brought was considered vital. After the economy grew rapidly following the Second World War, the number of people visiting Japan was considered to be of relatively small importance, in comparison to the manufacturing of electronics and automobiles which helped earn foreign currency.

But there has been a recent push to encourage people to visit Japan. Now Japanese industries, facing competition from countries like China, Korea, and Taiwan, in addition to the dominance of an internet-based economy coming from the United States, are losing their edge. Once, the Ministry of Economy, Trade and Industry (METI) was revered and feared as the engine of corporate Japan. Now, METI regards the 'soft power' of the nation as an indispensable part of its money-making machinery. METI has initiated a 'Cool Japan' campaign, inspired by the 'Cool Britannia' movement of the United Kingdom, which aims to encourage economies other than manufacturing, and secure tourism as the new breadwinner for the nation. To increase numbers of tourists is regarded as one of the important challenges of the 'Cool Japan' initiative.

Tourists often mention the high quality of service,

presentation and attention to detail as being some of the key charms of Japan. From the almost flawless operations of Shinkansen trains to the meticulously efficient and quick delivery of beef dishes in the fast food chains, things taken for granted by the Japanese tend to impress and even awe other nationalities. Visitors consistently find Japan clean and tidy, a place where everything works and is on time. Public toilets, convenience stores, and public transport in general are seen to be meticulously operated. Japanese locals are praised for being kind and helpful.

Needless to say, there are occasional hiccups; like everywhere, Japan has its share of incompetent people or organizations. The Japanese, always keen on maintaining a high standard, themselves often complain of deteriorating standards. But on average, it is fair to say that the Japanese would get an A+ when it comes to the general quality of services and friendliness.

When considering why Japan consistently delivers such high quality goods and services, it is important to understand the concept of *kodawari*.

Kodawari is a concept difficult to translate. In English it is often rendered as 'commitment' or 'insistence'. However, these words, like many concepts nurtured in a particular cultural context, do not adequately capture the true meaning of the word. *Kodawari* is a personal standard, to which the individual adheres in a steadfast manner. It is often, though not always, used in reference to a level of quality, or professionalism to which the individual holds. It is an attitude, often maintained throughout one's life, constituting a central element of *ikigai*. *Kodawari* is personal in nature, and it is a manifestation of a pride in what one does. In a nutshell, *kodawari* is an approach whereby you take extraordinary care of very small details. Of the Five Pillars of *ikigai*, *kodawari* is the first pillar, **starting small**, without necessarily justifying the effort for any grandiose schemes.

One thing visitors to Japan notice is the large number of small-scale restaurants and bars, owned and operated by private individuals rather than chains or conglomerates. They have a local feel, are unique, individual and represent their owners' tastes. These places will often have a *kodawari no ippin* — a particular signature dish — of which the owner is proud. It might involve specific ingredients, or focus on the region from which they've been sourced or on the amount of time taken to prepare the dish. Customers appreciate that these places where uniquely prepared dishes can be consumed are born from a wish to celebrate personal interaction and a sense of community.

A particularly interesting example is the famous *ramen* noodles. Here, Japan has shown great skill in transforming something imported from abroad into something close to perfection. This type of noodle originated in China, but once in Japan, there was an explosion in the kinds of *ramen* noodles produced. Depending on the flavour of the soup, how the noodle is prepared and the choice of ingredients, there is now a huge variety. Once two Japanese start arguing what kind of *ramen* noodles they like, you can be sure there will be no end to the discussion. One of the most astute cinematic observers of Japanese society, Juzo Itami, paid humorous tribute to the *kodawari* exhibited in *ramen* noodles in his film Tampopo (1985). Every aspect of *ramen* making, such as the concoction of soup, kneading of the noodles, and the number and proportions of toppings required is described. In addition, the customers have to learn the proper way to savour and eat *ramen*. This is all comically rendered in the film. But although the zeal bestowed on *ramen* is humorous and exaggerated, and there is much that is sheer entertainment, it is funny precisely because there is so much truth to it. **Starting small**, and executing each step to perfection is the very ethos of *ramen* shop owners in Japan, and one that is compassionately shared by the general public.

Kodawari in itself appears to be a trait that is uncompromising and self-centered, almost to the point of excluding all give and take. Indeed, in the popular imagination of the Japanese, a *ramen* shop owner with *kodawari* is hard to talk to, grumpy, demanding the same standard of appreciation on the part of the customers. In *Tampopo*, the *ramen* shop owner is only satisfied when his customers have drunk all the soup. But in actual fact, *kodawari* is ultimately all about communication. The final and personal reward for performing each of the small tasks that go into making the perfect bowl of *ramen* is the smile on the customer's face.

Steve Jobs had this kind of *kodawari* too, although he didn't express his ethos in so many words, when he tried to perfect the features of the iPhone, for example. In fact, one may say that *kodawari* was Steve Jobs's defining characteristic. One could even say that Steve Jobs was a Japanese in his *kodawari* spirit!

Of course, Jobs was an outstanding individual. What is perhaps unique in Japan is the prevalence of the *kodawari* spirit among ordinary people. From small owners of *izakaya* taverns to producers of Kobe beef and tuna from Ōma (a port in the Aomori prefecture, in the north of the country), Japan has a large population of people expressing their own *kodawari*. There are many artisanal farmers who devote all their time, efforts and ingenuity to creating the best and tastiest produce. They get the soil right, plan and execute optimum pruning and watering, and choose the variety of produce to be planted very carefully. They go an incredible length, propelled by their strong sense of **starting small.**

One crucial aspect of *kodawari* is that people pursue their own goals above and beyond reasonable expectations based on market forces.

If you want to succeed, you usually need to produce items of reasonable quality. However, once you reach a certain level, the incremental improvement in quality diminishes compared to the input of effort. It is like the learning curve. If you are a student, at a certain point, it does not make sense to study further except in unusual circumstances, since the improvement in score is small; you are better advised to put your effort into something else.

This kind of rationality is alien for people who have *kodawari*. They are not satisfied with 'just fine' *ramen* noodle. They will not stop the pursuit of quality with 'just so' tuna (remember Fujita). Producing 'just fine' or 'just so' things would make you reasonably successful. However, those with *kodawari* go beyond that, without any apparent reason. 'Good enough' is simply not 'good enough' for them. You could even call it a creative insanity, really.

At a certain point, a casual observer might feel that these pursuers of perfection are going over the top, and that the effort is too much. Just at that moment, something miraculous happens. You realize that there is actually further depth to the quality you are pursuing. There is a breakthrough, or the production of something completely different. With the creation of a new genre of products a brand new market emerges, in which people are prepared to pay premium prices for qualities previously unimagined.

For example, producing fruit is a field in which the Japanese have exhibited a particularly high degree of *kodawari*. Fruit producers aim for ever better quality. Some people even pursue the dream of a 'perfect fruit', for example, a strawberry which has a gradient of sweet and sour along the longitudinal axis.

One of the most interesting features of the perfect fruits offered at Sembikiya, Japan's premium fruit shop, however, is that there is no single definition of 'perfect'. Just looking at the strawberry section, you have a feeling that you are witnessing the culmination of different lines of evolution, which do not necessarily lead to any single definition of what a strawberry should taste and look like.

In Japan, there is even an elite league of fruits. Sembikiya dates back to 1834. The fruit sold there is of such supreme quality that if a produce is accepted to be sold in one of its shops, it can be considered to have made it to the hall of fame for fruits. When you visit one of the Sembikiya outlets in or out of Tokyo, it is difficult not to be impressed by the incredibly high prices and the beautiful appearance of the fruits, which are almost like works of fine art.

A quintessential example of the perfect fruit sold there is the muskmelon, named after its particular musk flavour. The very mention of Sembikiya conjures up an image of a muskmelon in the public's imagination with extraordinarily high prices, usually purchased for gifts. Indeed, in Japan, a gift of a muskmelon is considered the highest expression of respect. A Sembikiya muskmelon can cost you anything from 20,000 yen ($200) upwards a piece. It may sound ridiculous, but if you knew the extreme efforts – and the *kodawari* – that go into the making of a muskmelon, you might, incredibly, think it is a bargain.

Muskmelons sold in Sembikiya are grown with the 'one stalk one fruit' method, by which the superfluous fruits are removed, so that they don't take away the nutrients that go into the one targeted fruit. Because people know the extraordinary efforts that go into the making of a muskmelon, they don't consider the price tag ridiculous, although, needless to say, not everyone can afford it.

If you are lucky enough to receive a Sembikiya muskmelon

as a gift, prepare yourself for a whole new experience in sweet, juicy, and sublime flavour and texture. If you cannot afford the whole fruit, you can taste slices offered at the cafés and restaurants operated by Sembikiya, where they use the same muskmelons sold at the outlets.

The fruit sold at Sembikiya are biological arts produced by the *kodawari* of dedicated farmers. Needless to say, the proof of these arts is in the eating. You might admire a *kanjuku* (perfectly ripe) mango, priced at over 10,000 yen ($100) a piece. The mango would appear as a jewel in the shiny presentation box specially prepared by Sembikiya. The incredibly high price would make you shy to tamper with it, let alone consume it. However, unless you skin the fruit, cut it into pieces, you cannot appreciate the true value of the perfect ripe mango. In other words, you need to destroy it, in order to appreciate it.

And how subtle that experience is! You put the fruit into your mouth, munch and swallow it, and then, it's gone. Your $100-worth gourmet experience is over.

Perhaps the Japanese love affair with the perfect fruit is a reflection of a belief in the ephemeral. *Hanami*, when the

Japanese admire the blooming of the cherry blossoms every spring, is a prime example. The Japanese take the transient things of life seriously. The eating of a perfect mango or stately muskmelon takes only a few minutes, providing a fleeting joy. You cannot hold on to the experience. Unlike audiovisual stimuli, there is no record of what you eat, and that is how it is likely to remain for the foreseeable future. You can't take a selfie of taste!

The belief in the ephemeral of *ikigai*, **being in the here and now** (the fifth pillar), is possibly the most profound of the Five Pillars.

Of course, ephemeral joy is not necessarily a trademark of Japan. For example, the French take sensory pleasures seriously. So do the Italians. Or, for that matter, the Russians, the Chinese, or even the English. Every culture has its own inspiration to offer.

But here's another example of *kodawari* in Japanese culture: pottery.

The Japanese have always appreciated the art of pottery. Bowls used in tea ceremonies have been particularly valued for centuries. When the warlords fought in battles and made their names, they expected to receive famous bowls as symbolic rewards. It is even said that some warlords were disappointed when they received only a castle and land to govern, rather than a precious bowl.

There is a particularly famous type of bowl that used to be treasured by the warlords, called *yohen tenmoku*. *Yohen* refers to the concept of metamorphosis in the process of baking pottery in the kiln. *Yohen tenmoku* bowls are thought to have been produced in China in the period of a few hundred years starting in the tenth century. *Tenmoku* is the Japanese pronunciation of Tianmu, a famous mountain west of Hangzhou in China from where, it is believed, certain types of bowls originated.

A *yohen tenmoku* bowl exhibits a star-like pattern of deep blue, purple and other colours, like a galaxy of luminance scattered in the black expansion of the cosmos, which is why I call it, quite simply, 'starry bowl'. There remain only three starry bowls in the world. All of them are in Japan, and each one is registered as a National Treasure. Each one is unlike the other – they have an unmistakable individuality, and leave an unforgettable impression.

Legends abound about treasured bowls in Japan, but the one about starry bowls is particularly poignant. Historically, there was a fourth starry bowl, treasured by the legendary warlord Nobunaga Oda. It is believed to have been destroyed when Nobunaga Oda met his untimely death in 1582 by his retainer Mitsuhide Akechi at the Honnō-ji temple in Kyoto, in a *coup d'état*, just as expectations were mounting for Oda to reunite Japan after the chaos caused by the Ōnin War that had lasted for more than a hundred years. Taken by surprise, and seeing there was no chance of winning or escape, the proud Oda killed himself, and set the temple on fire, destroying everything, including the prized bowl.

Today, how the starry bowl was made is regarded as one of the greatest mysteries in the history of pottery making. It is generally regarded that they were made from feldspar, limestone and iron oxide. Depending on the way the clay is prepared, and how the ceramic glaze is formed and finished in the process of heating and cooling, bowls exhibit variable surface patterns and textures. These bowls are remarkable for the variability of their finish, an alchemic process of transformation that is not perfectly understood or controlled by craftsmen. Within that vast universe of possible patterns reside the starry bowls, which are likely to have been produced as the result of rare chance. The probability of the production of a starry bowl was perhaps less than one in tens of thousands of specimens.

The reproduction of the starry bowl has become the passion and *kodawari* of some famous pottery makers in Japan. They love this precious bowl so much that its reproduction has become their life-long passion. It now represents the holy grail of Japanese pot making.

One of them is Soukichi Nagae the 9th, who is the ninth-generation master of a pot-making household based in the city of Seto near Nagoya, an area that Nobunaga Oda used to govern. Nagae is the family name, while 'Soukichi' is the designated common name assumed by the masters of the house.

The reproduction of the starry bowl was originally a passion of his father, Soukichi Nagae the 8th. Soukichi Nagae the 9th testifies that his father was a 'once started, he would bet his life on it' kind of man. While his father was alive, since childhood, he heard the name 'starry bowl' mentioned tens of thousands of times, literally filling their daily lives. Indeed, his father was so captivated by the pursuit of the starry bowl that, for a period, he abandoned his day job, which was the production of conventional Seto pottery.

Soukichi Nagae the 8th made some progress, and at one point it looked as though success was in sight. Then the long stalemate began. Without completing the reproduction of the starry bowl, he passed away, suffering a stroke. Nagae, after assuming the title of Soukichi Nagae the 9th, initiated his own efforts to reproduce the bowl. He bought more than a hundred different materials for pot making, and tried different combinations, with variable proportions. Nagae tried more than 700 kinds of *yuyaku*, a special cocktail of materials used to cover the pot before putting it through the baking process.

The starry bowls are thought to have been made in Jian ware furnaces of the Fujian province of China. There used to be around ten furnaces in the district producing Jian ware, and it seems most likely that the starry bowls were made in one of them. One of the furnaces that has been excavated in modern times measured a length of 135 metres, and more than 100,000 pots would have been put in it over the years. The Jian ware site was used for more than 300 years, from around the tenth to the thirteenth centuries AD. The starry bowls would have been one of millions of pots produced there.

Soukichi Nagae the 9th imported a container full of soil from the Jian ware site which weighed forty tons, or the equivalent of material for 10,000 bowls. Making bowls from the Jian ware soil had been a dream handed down from his father, Soukichi Nagae the 8th. For Nagae, the replicating of a starry bowl was like building a pyramid. At the pinnacle, you will find the starry bowls. However, you have to level the ground first, in order to make the ascent possible.

At the Jian ware site, there still remain mountains of failed pots. Layers of broken pieces, at times more than ten metres deep, cover an area of twelve hectares. Strangely, a starry bowl fragment has never been discovered there. This has led to various speculations, including some conspiracy theories.

However, in 2009, fragments of a starry bowl were discovered in a construction site in the city of Hangzhou, which used to be the de facto capital of the Southern Song dynasty (1127–1279), effectively putting an end to conspiracy theories. It is now thought that starry bowls were indeed produced by craftsmen in the Jian ware district.

In 2002, Soukichi Nagae the 9th made a presentation in an international symposium held in Jingdezhen, a city which has produced pottery for 1,700 years and which is known as the 'porcelain capital'. In this presentation, Nagae laid out the fundamentals of his approach towards replicating these ancient pots. Nagae hypothesized that the use and vaporization of fluorite in the Jian ware kilns contributed to the formation of various *tenmoku* ware patterns, including those of the starry bowls.

Today there are some hopeful-looking signs of success in the reproduction of starry bowls, but the quest of Nagae and others is far from over.

The story of the starry bowls is characteristic of the Japanese mindset in several ways. The first characteristic is the great curiosity exhibited towards things that come from abroad, such as these bowls from China. As already mentioned, all three starry bowls that remain in Japan are designated National Treasures by the Agency of Cultural

Affairs, a governmental organization dealing with such matters. There are numerous other examples where artifacts originating in other countries are highly valued and given status of the highest recognition by the Japanese government. The denomination 'National' Treasure has nothing to do with chauvinistic nationalism.

The people of Japan are good at absorbing and then adapting and owning something that has been imported, whether Chinese characters in ancient times or the techniques used to make the English garden in recent years. Baseball was imported from the United States, and has evolved into a Japanese sport with quite distinct characteristics. Take *Anne of Green Gables* by the Canadian novelist Lucy Maud Montgomery, or *Moomin* by the Finnish author Tove Jansson. Both books have been made into successful anime series. The novelist Haruki Murakami has been translating works written in English, most notably those by Raymond Carver. Due to the reputation of the novelist himself, and partly because of the quality of the translation, translated authors have grown to be quite popular amongst Japanese readers, with an almost cult following.

As we have seen in this chapter, the Japanese are some-times dedicated to producing things with an attention so meticulous that it verges on the ridiculous, such as the perfect fruit sold at Sembikiya or attempts to reproduce the starry bowl. *Ikigai* derived from living up to one's *kodawari* is often the engine behind these actions. If you take *kodawari* in the static sense, it might sometimes appear to lead to an inflex-ibility of method, an emphasis on tradition and a closing of the mind to external influences. However, as we have seen thus far, *kodawari* does not necessarily lead to a rejection of external influences. Quite the contrary, the Japanese have been and still are curious people.

Crucially, **starting small** is the hallmark of youthful days. When you are young, you cannot start things in a big way. Whatever you do, it does not matter much to the world. You need to start small. And what you have in abundance is open-mindedness and curiosity, the great kick-starters devoted to one's cause. Children are always so inquisitive, you can see what the link is between curiosity and *ikigai*.

Funnily enough, in postwar Japan, the Supreme Com-mander of the Allied Powers, General Douglas MacArthur (who was the leader of the nation as the top military governor at GHQ), famously referred to Japan as 'a nation of twelve-year olds'. In this remark, MacArthur referred to the immature nature of Japan's democracy at that time. The phrase was intended to be derogatory. However, if you take the view that a youthful mindset with its avid expression of curiosity is a plus in life, then MacArthur's remark could be taken as a compliment.

Just possibly, *ikigai* makes a Peter Pan of all of us. And that is not necessarily a bad thing. Let us all be twelve years old!

Youthfulness of mind is important in *ikigai*, but so is commitment and passion, however seemingly insignificant your goal is.

CHAPTER 4

The sensory beauty of *ikigai*

A starry bowl in good condition, if put in an auction, would fetch millions of dollars. Of the ones that remain, the Inaba starry bowl (*inaba tenmoku*) is regarded as the finest of the three. It was handed down from the Tokugawa Shogunate to the house of Inaba, and would fetch tens of millions of dollars if put on the market today.

Koyata Iwasaki, the fourth president of Mitsubishi Conglomerate, and one of the richest men in modern Japan, became the owner of that particular bowl in 1934. However, considering himself unworthy of it, Iwasaki never used it at his tea ceremonies.

The Japanese certainly make a fuss of pretty bowls. After all, a bowl is just a bowl, and its function is to contain liquid.

In terms of that capacity, it is no different from any ordinary bowl in the market. And while the enthusiasm surrounding these receptacles would surely find parallels in other cultures, one feels that there is something unique in the Japanese culture that makes the passion for them quite extraordinary. Where does this kind of sensory enthusiasm come from?

In Chapter 1, we referred to the lexical hypothesis, which states that expressions for important personality traits in life gradually and eventually come to constitute a part of everyday language, as is the case with *ikigai*. There is another interesting aspect of the Japanese language, worth focusing on and particularly pertinent here.

In Japanese, a dog barks *wan wan*, while a cat goes *nya nya*. In English, they go bow-wow and meow respectively. Every language has its share of such onomatopoeic expressions, but it is generally considered that the Japanese language has an inordinately abundant variety of them.

They are sometimes referred to as Japanese sound symbolism, and they are often made up of the same word said twice.

For example, *bura bura* means a nonchalant, carefree way

of walking, while *teka teka* describes a shiny surface. *Kira kira* refers to the glittering of light, whereas *gira gira* refers to a more intense, almost blinding source of light, such as the headlight of a motorbike at night. *Ton ton* refers to a light tapping sound, whereas *don don* refers to a heavy, thudding one. A dictionary of onomatopoeia edited by Masahiro Ono (2007) lists 4,500 instances of sound symbolism.

With the growing popularity of Japanese manga and anime, an increasing number of people around the world are interested in Japanese sound symbolism, as many of the expressions are frequently used in popular manga and anime works. However, Japanese onomatopoeia is difficult to master, partly because of the subtlety in the way it is used and partly because there is so much of it. Unlike in some cultures, the Japanese continue to use sound symbolism in their adult life, as well as in childhood. Indeed, it is not uncommon for the Japanese to use sound symbolism when discussing things in a professional context. Such a perception structure has certainly developed more in some fields of industry than others, for example, in gastronomy. You can imagine sushi chefs such as Ono Jiro and experienced fish brokers such as Hiroki Fujita using onomatopoeia in their conversation, because sound symbolism is often used to describe the texture and flavour of food. Similarly, you can be sure samurai warriors used onomatopoeia to discuss the quality of swords, from the glitter to the texture of the blade surface. Manga artists make frequent use of it too, using words such as *ton ton* and *don don* to reflect the subtle nuances of the actions of their characters.

The fact that there is so much sound symbolism in the Japanese language implies, according to the lexical hypothesis, that there is a correlation between it and the way in which the Japanese perceive the world. The Japanese seem to distinguish between many different nuances of experience, paying attention to the plethora of sensory qualities. The proliferation of onomatopoeia reflects the importance of detailed sensory nuances in the life of the Japanese.

Such attention to detail has nurtured a culture in which craftspeople continue to receive respect, in an era where waves of innovation promise to change our lives.

Japan continues to have a large number of traditional products made by craftspeople. Craftspeople, although not outspoken or flamboyant, are held in high esteem and play pivotal roles in Japanese society. Often, their lives are regarded as the embodiment of *ikigai* – lives devoted to creating just one thing properly, however small.

The work of craftspeople is often very labour-intensive and time-consuming. As a result, the product tends to be highly refined and of excellent quality. Japanese consumers recognize that time and effort has gone into the creation of these goods and appreciate the quality, in such diverse areas as the crafting of knives, swords, blades, ceramics, lacquerware, *washi* paper, and of weaving.

The ethics and work of craftspeople continue to have an impact on a wide range of economic activities. Similarly, the Japanese understanding and handling of the great variety of sensory qualities have led to correspondingly fine artisanship and manufacturing techniques.

Although Japanese companies have been losing out for many years in the field of consumer electronics, one area in which the Japanese are still preeminent is the manufacturing of intricate instruments such as medical cameras. High-end precision engineering and commitment to perfection makes

Japanese medical cameras among the best in the world. Likewise, in the case of semiconductor devices, Japanese manufacturers have the advantage, the accumulation of knowhow and carefully coordinated operations being a must for efficient and high quality production.

Paying attention to the multitude of sensory experiences is necessary to execute the finely tuned operations supporting craftsmanship and high-tech manufacturing. As with craftsmanship, these cognitive capabilities are reflected in the linguistic make-up of the language. The richness of the Japanese language as regards onomatopoeia reflects such fine-tuned sensitivities.

As we will see later in Chapter 8, in the Japanese mind, each sensory quality is equivalent to a god. The Japanese tend to believe that there is an infinite depth to the nuances displayed by the multitudes of colours in nature and artifacts, just as the story of God creating the whole universe is deep.

Sei Shōnagon, a court lady who served Empress Teishi around the year 1000, is famous for her collection of essays *Makura no soshi* (*The Pillow Book*). In one essay, Sei Shōnagon pays meticulous attention to the small things in life. Here's an example (my own translation): 'Cute things. A child's face painted on a melon. A young sparrow hopping towards an imitated mouse squeal. A toddler crawling in a hurry, finding a small piece of dust, and pinching it with lovely fingers, and showing it to adults.'

Sei Shōnagon does not use grandiose words to describe life. She just pays attention to the small things she encounters in life, understanding instinctively the importance of **being in the here and now**. Sei Shōnagon also does not talk about herself. Referring to small things that surround her gives an expression of her own individuality much more effectively than a direct reference to her person.

Sei Shōnagon's approach as expressed in *The Pillow Book* can be linked to the contemporary concept of 'mindfulness'. In order to practise mindfulness, it is important to attend to the **here and now**, without rushing to make judgements. An adherence to the self is considered to stand in the way of achieving mindfulness.

Considering when *The Pillow Book* was written (it was completed in 1002 AD), the fundamentally secular nature of the essays foretell of the contemporary *zeitgeist* by a millennium. It is almost as though the author, Sei Shōnagon, belongs to modern times.

One of the unique Japanese contributions to the philosophy of life, as it applies to the meaning of life, therefore, would perhaps come from a negation of the self.

A carefree child does not need *ikigai* to carry on, a point stressed by Mieko Kamiya in her famous book *On the Meaning of Life (ikigai)*. A carefree child is not burdened with a social definition of the self. A child is not tied to a specific profession, nor social status, yet. It would be wonderful to maintain a child's way throughout one's life. This leads to the second pillar of *ikigai*, **releasing oneself.**

Just as Sei Shōnagon almost never refers to her own position in society in the whole of *The Pillow Book* as if she was born just this morning, like virgin snow falling on the ground, forgetting oneself leads us to one of the key tenets of Zen Buddhism. It is interesting to observe how self-negation goes hand in hand with the appreciation of the present, in a fulfilment of mindfulness philosophy. **Releasing oneself** is very much related to **being in the here and now**. After all, it was in the traditions of Buddhist meditation that the modern concept of mindfulness was born.

The Eihei-ji temple in the suburb of Fukui, Japan is one of the centres of excellence for Zen Buddhism. Founded in 1244 by Dōgen, the Eihei-ji temple remains fully operational today, as the venue for the learning and training of would-be priests. Thousands of candidates for the priesthood have applied to and studied at the temple, to train, meditate and obtain qualifications. In order to be accepted as a disciple at the temple, an applicant must stand in front of the gate for days, sometimes in the pouring rain. Although it might seem to be abuse from the modern point of view, there is a rationale as to why such a demeaning introduction to the world of Zen is considered necessary, especially with regard to the negation of the self.

Jikisai Minami is a Buddhist priest who had the rare experience of staying within the realm of the Eihei-ji temple for more than ten years (most disciples stay only a few years in order to qualify). Minami says that one of the most important rules of the Eihei-ji temple (and therefore Zen Buddhism in general) is that there is no 'merit system'. In the outside world, people get credits, or brownie points, for doing something valuable, something good. Within the Eihei-ji temple, however, there is no redeeming prize for a laudable act. Once you get into the system, no matter what you do, however earnestly you may meditate, however conscientiously you might execute the daily chores, it does not make any difference. You are treated like any other regular disciple: you become an anonymous being, almost invisible; individuality loses any sense of relevance.

The schedule at the Eihei-ji temple is very arduous. The disciples get up at 3.00 am, and after cleaning themselves, practise morning meditation. After the meditation comes a heavy schedule consisting of more meditation, cleaning and various chores. The disciples take three meals a day. The menu is very simple, consisting of rice, soup, and a few vegetarian items.

During the day, the Eihei-ji temple is open to the public, and tourists can wander around in the interior. The disciples share the same space as the tourists. From time to time, it happens that tourists encounter disciples walking along the corridors. The contrast between the countenances of the tourists and disciples could not be greater. The tourists bring the air of the wider world, with its emphasis on self-aware-ness, the pressure to make good use of one's self, effectively to collect brownie points. The disciples, on the other hand, walk by as if they are not aware of their own presence, let alone that of others. They have succeeded in the **releasing oneself** pillar of *ikigai*. They are slim, with smooth skins (it is said that the Eihei-ji diet is good for facial beauty), and they exhibit a deep self-absorption which can make even an onlooker feel envious.

In fact, imagine for a moment that you are one of the disciples in the Eihei-ji temple. The sensory flow in your mind is filled with the exquisite architecture, interior and other beauties that have been designed, maintained and polished over the years. Although your material satisfaction would be minimal, and there would be no satisfaction for the ego, every waking moment spent at Eihei-ji would be an unbroken flow of sensory beauty.

When you are immersed in the ambience of the temple, you have a sense of almost timeless bliss. As if to compen-sate for the loss of individuality and the merit system, there is an abundance of serene beauty within the temple, providing the setting in which the disciples carry out these daily rituals.

The Cambridge (UK) based neuroscientist Nicholas Humphrey, who discussed the functional significance of consciousness in his book *Soul Dust: the Magic of Consciousness*, argues that consciousness is functionally significant because it gives us sensory pleasure – a reason to carry on with life.

Humphrey takes up the extraordinary example of the ritual of the prisoners' last breakfast before their execution in the United States. The prisoners have the final privilege of choosing their own personal menu. Humphrey quotes the prisoner's last menu as posted on the Texas Department of Criminal Justice website. One inmate might select fried fish fillet, French fries, orange juice, German chocolate cake, another might go for a plate of chicken katsu. The point is that they give considerable thought to the very last meal of their life, a testimony of the importance of the sensory pleasures we derive from our food. It can be said to be an ultimate form of **being in the here and now**. It is almost as though finding *ikigai* in a given environment could be regarded as a form of biological adaptation. You could find your *ikigai* in a wide range of conditions, and the key to that resilience is sensory pleasure.

In the contemporary science of consciousness, sensory qualities that accompany an experience, including those in culinary consumption, are called 'qualia'. The term refers to the phenomenological properties of sensory experience: the redness of red, the fragrance of a rose or the coolness of water are all examples of qualia. How qualia arise from the activities of neurons in the brain is the greatest unsolved mystery in neuroscience, or, indeed, in the whole of science. Nothing turns us on like a great mystery. If you put a strawberry in your mouth (it does not have to be one of the expensive perfect fruits sold at Sembikiya), you have a certain spectrum of qualia, which would presumably give you pleasure. And the pleasure is equal to the mystery of life.

Earlier, we drew our attention to the fact that there are many examples of onomatopoeia (sound symbolism) in the Japanese language. Onomatopoeia, after all, is just representation of various qualia encountered in life.

There is a deep link here. In a mysterious way, **releasing**

oneself is linked to the discovery of the sensory pleasures. The Japanese culture, with its abundance of onomatopoeia, has cultivated this linkage, nurturing a very robust system of *ikigai* in its course. By relieving ourselves of the burden of the self, we can open up to the infinite universe of sensory pleasures.

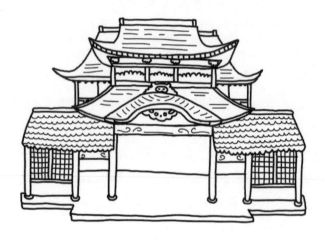

CHAPTER 5

Flow and creativity

Negation of the self sounds a little pejorative. It conjures up thoughts of denial and rejection. However, if you understand the beneficial repercussions that come with this approach within the context of *ikigai*, nothing becomes more positive.

If you can achieve the psychological state of 'flow', as described by the Hungarian-born American psychologist Mihaly Csikszentmihalyi, you will get the most out of *ikigai*, and things such as daily chores will even become enjoyable. You won't feel the need to have your work or efforts recognized, you won't be looking for a reward of any sort. The idea of living in a continuous state of bliss, without searching for immediate gratification through external recognition, is suddenly within your reach.

According to Csikszentmihalyi, flow is a state in which

people are so involved in an activity that nothing else seems to matter. That is how you find pleasure in work. Work becomes an end in itself, rather than something to be endured as a means of achieving something. When in flow, you don't work to earn money for your living. At least, that is not your first priority. You work, because working itself gives you immense pleasure. Wages are a bonus.

Negation of the self, therefore, becomes a release from the burden of the self and becomes a fundamental aspect of flow. It corresponds to the second pillar of *ikigai*, which is **releasing oneself**. Naturally, as a biological entity, you are concerned about your own welfare, the satisfaction of your desires. That is normal. However, in order to achieve this state, you need to release your ego. After all, it is not the ego that is important. It is the accumulation of the infinite nuances of the elements involved in a work that are important. You are not the master, work is the master, and in flow you can identify yourself with your work in a joyous, symbiotic way. A serious pursuit of personal objective is not unknown in Japan. Life is about coherence, and it helps to have a sense of direction, a vision of life's goals, even when one has small things to support one's *ikigai*. Indeed, coherence and a sense of life's goals ultimately make small pieces of *ikigai* shine.

Among those who treasure antique porcelain in Japan, it is sometimes said that 'unconscious creation' produces the best masterpieces. It is argued that in modern times artists have become too aware of their individuality. In olden times, artists did not make their products to claim their rights as creators. They just did their job, expecting nothing more than that people would find these wares useful in their daily lives. The porcelain remaining from ancient times exhibits a state of purity and sincerity not to be found nowadays, say the connoisseurs. There are anonymous expressions of beauty in these wares.

Being in a state of flow, released from the burden of the self, shows in the quality of the work. The beauty of the starry bowls is so sublime precisely because these items were products of unconscious endeavour. One could argue that modern attempts to reproduce starry bowls have fallen short of reproducing the serene beauty of the antiques, because of the conscious action of wanting to create something beautiful and unique. We perhaps intuitively know the truth of this view. In a world obsessed with selfies, self-help and self-promotions, this principle feels all the more pertinent.

Japanese anime are now world famous. However, it is also common knowledge that the animators are not well paid. Compared to more practical jobs such as banking and retail, the wage of the average animator is meagre. Despite that, working as an animator continues to be many youngsters' dream job. Knowing perfectly well that they will not be able to make a fortune, generations after generations of would-be animators flock to the studios.

Making anime is a tough job. For Hayao Miyazaki, the great master of Japanese animation known for works such as *Spirited Away* and *My Neighbor Totoro*, film making means long hours of hard labour. Miyazaki never stirs from his desk, drawing thousands of sketches which define the characters and designate the scenes; and these are then worked on and refined by animators of Studio Ghibli, the company which he co-founded.

I once had the immense pleasure of interviewing Hayao Miyazaki at Studio Ghibli. He has received numerous accolades but, judging from his remarks, the real rewards of his work come from the act of anime making itself. Hayao Miyazaki makes anime in a state of flow, and it shows. You simply feel the quality of bliss emanating from his works. A child is a consumer of absolute honesty. You cannot impose something on a child, no matter how educationally valuable you may deem it to be. Therefore, the fact that a child, when shown a Studio Ghibli anime work, voluntarily keeps watching, begging for more, is a great testimony to the quality of films made by Hayao Miyazaki.

My theory is that this man understands the psychology of a child, perhaps because he has an inner child alive in himself. Being in the flow is all about treasuring the **being in the here and now**. A child knows the value of being in the present. Actually, a child has no definite idea of the past or the future. His or her happiness resides in the present, as does Miyazaki's.

Miyazaki told me a story that left a strong and lasting impression on me. Once, he said, a five-year-old child came to visit Studio Ghibli. After the child played for some time at the studios, Miyazaki took the child and his parent to the nearest station. At that time, Miyazaki owned a car with a convertible hood. 'This child would love a ride with the roof down', Miyazaki thought. Just as he was trying to lower the roof, however, a light rain began to fall. 'Maybe next time,' Miyazaki judged, and drove to the station with the roof remaining shut.

Sometime later, Miyazaki said, he began to have a sense of remorse. He realized that, for a child, a day is a day, and it never returns. A child grows out of himself so rapidly. Even if the child returns one year later, and is taken on a ride with the roof open, it is not the same thing. In other words, the precious moment had been lost forever, and because of Miyazaki's oversight.

Miyazaki's words were very sincere, and I was deeply moved. If ever there needed to be proof of the existence of Miyazaki's ability to put himself in the position of a child and produce masterpiece after masterpiece of anime that would bewitch them, there it was. Miyazaki has kept his inner child alive. The most important characteristic of a child's existence is living in the present, here and now. The same attitude is vital for the creative life.

In a sense, Walt Disney was another evangelist of **being in the here and now**. He would have made animation in a state of flow, too, judging from the sheer quality of the legacy he left behind. Despite his huge success – fifty-nine Oscar nominations and twenty-two Oscars – he could never have reached those heady heights without wanting to immerse himself in the time-consuming and excessively intricate job of animation itself. Once, Disney was told by someone that he was popular enough to become president. Why on earth would he want to be president, Walt retorted, when he was already the king of Disneyland?

Today, many people, young and old, experience flow while watching a Disney animation, or enjoying a ride in Disneyland. Perhaps the greatest legacy of Walt Disney was making the flow experience tangible and sustainable, so that it could be shared by millions of ordinary people, who might otherwise have lost the magic of childhood forever.

In the context of the flow, or the relation between work and the self, the Japanese attitude is perhaps unique, at least compared to the standard concept in the West. People such as Disney are an exception. Because unlike in the Christian tradition, where labour tends to be regarded as a necessary evil (metaphorically a result of the expulsion of Adam and Eve from the Garden of Eden due to Original Sin), the Japanese embrace work as something of positive value in itself. The attitude towards retirement is different in Japan; there salaried workers look forward to doing some work even after they reach their company's designated retirement age – and not because they are at a loss for something to do.

Although Japanese working conditions are probably far from perfect, many people enjoy working as opposed to retiring. Being in the state of flow makes working sustainable and enjoyable. It is well known that Hayao Miyazaki has announced his 'retirement' in the past, only to resume work on a feature-length animation (which involves a lot of labour) later. The latest retirement announcement came after the completion of *The Wind Rises* in 2013, prompting many to consider this the great director's swan song. However, at the time of writing, rumour has it that Hayao Miyazaki is at it again, working on a feature-length anime project. It appears that Miyazaki simply cannot be separated from the workplace.

Csikszentmihalyi testifies that one source of inspiration for his work on flow came when he observed a painter friend working on his artwork for hours on end, without any prospect of selling the work or getting financial reward for it. This particular state of mind, or work ethic, where you just immerse yourself in the joy of **being in the here and now**, without asking for immediate reward or recognition, is an integral part of the Japanese concept of *ikigai*.

Let us look at the business of making Japanese whisky. You will see that the production of whisky in Japan is a surprising example of the fundamentally positive attitude towards labour. It is a labour of love, coupled with the negation of the self. It also has a lot of resonance with the state of flow.

When you think about it, there is no reason for Japan to make whisky. The country does not grow barley; it does not have peat. However, for decades the Japanese have dedicated themselves to the task of creating excellent whisky, and now they produce internationally recognized, award-winning spirits. Some whisky experts even go so far as to count Japanese whisky among the five major whiskies in the world, along with Scotch, Irish, Bourbon and Canadian.

Take Ichiro Akuto, who operates modest premises with just two tiny pot stills in the hills of Chichibu. The Akuto family has been producing *sake*, Japan's traditional alcoholic drink, since 1625. It was in 2004 that Ichiro Akuto decided to start producing whisky, with the new distillery being completed in 2007. The first release of Chichibu single malt was in 2011. Despite this very recent entry into the competitive whisky market, Akuto's whisky is already very highly regarded in the world market, and receives rave reviews. The Playing Card series comprised 54 single malt whiskies, each with a distinct label featuring a playing card, and was released over a period of several years. The complete set fetched a price of about $4,000,000 in Hong Kong. Akuto's single malt whisky, released under the brand name 'Ichiro's Malt', also fetches high prices. Many regard Ichiro Akuto as the new rising star in the world of whisky making.

Seiichi Koshimizu, the chief blender of Suntory, the Japanese brewing and distilling group, has been involved in the intricate art of finding the perfect blend for many years. He has been responsible for the blending of premium brands such as Hibiki, and has won numerous awards. But the fruits of his intricate works often become apparent only after decades. Koshimizu, now at the mature age of sixty-eight, might never get to see how the fruits of his current labour will turn out.

Koshimizu is a man of self-imposed customs. He eats exactly the same menu (*udon* noodle soup) for lunch every day, in order not to disturb the all-important tasting capacities of his tongue. His main weapon is his steadfast reliability, unmovable like the barrels that remain still in the rack house to mature the whisky.

He once told me an interesting philosophy about whisky blending. It is not possible, he said, to predict how a whisky in a particular barrel will evolve over the years. Even if you put the same whisky in similar oak barrels, it will mature into different flavours and taste after years of being kept in stock. According to him, it may happen that the character of whisky matured in a particular barrel is too strong to be enjoyed by itself. When blended with other whiskies, however, the strong character will be diluted and can give a surprisingly satisfying finish to the blended whisky.

Isn't it interesting how an element, which might not be

appreciated by itself, turns out to contribute to the overall quality when blended with elements of different characters? It is like the essence of life itself. The complex interaction between various elements in an organic system makes life robust and sustainable.

The Japanese interest in wine is more recent, but today we are seeing the same process at work, with many small producers seeking to create wine of world standard. There is a common theme to whisky and wine making – the importance of working patiently for many years, without expectations of immediate reward or recognition. Perhaps that is something that the Japanese are good at, with help from a robust sense of *ikigai*.

Being in a sense of flow is important to making your job an enjoyable one, but, at the same time, attention to detail must exist, in order to improve the quality of job done.

Being immersed in and drawing pleasure from the here and now, and attending to the smallest detail while doing so, is the essence of the mastery of the tea ceremony. It is extraordinary that Sen no Rikyū, the founder of the tea ceremony who lived in the sixteenth century, arrived at this concept in the Sengoku era, when the samurai warlords fought each other in endless battle after endless battle, and in what was presumably a very stressful time to live.

Tai-an, the only remaining tea house designed by Sen no Rikyū, is very small, with barely enough room to seat the tea master and a few guests. The tea house was intentionally designed to be compact so that the samurai warriors, who were the main guests at the tea ceremony, could have an intimate conversation. The samurais had to leave their swords at the entrance, as there was quite intentionally no room for their weapons. They even had to twist their bodies and bow low to get in.

The Japanese concept, *ichigo ichie* (literally meaning 'one time, one encounter') originally comes from the tea ceremony tradition. Rikyū is the most likely originator of this important idea. *Ichigo ichie* is the appreciation of the ephemeral character of any encounters with people, things or events in life. Precisely because an encounter is ephemeral, it must be taken seriously. Life, after all, is filled with things that happen only once. The realization of the 'onceness' of life's encounters and pleasures provides the foundations for the

Japanese conceptualization of *ikigai*, and is central to the Japanese philosophy of life. When you take notice of the small details of life, nothing is repeated. Every opportunity is special. That is why the Japanese treat the tiniest detail of any ritual as if it were a question of life and death.

The tradition of the tea ceremony is very much alive today. Indeed, this tradition is interesting in that all Five Pillars of *ikigai* seem to be embodied within it. In a tea ceremony, the master carefully prepares the ornaments in the room, paying the utmost attention to details such as the kind of flower to be decorated on the wall (**starting small**). The spirit of humility is the hallmark of the tea master and the guests, even if they have long years of experience in the ceremony (**releasing oneself**). Many wares used in a tea ceremony are decades, sometimes even centuries old, and are chosen so that they resonate with each other to leave an unforgettable impression (**harmony and sustainability**). Despite the meticulous preparations, the utmost goal of a tea ceremony is to be relaxed, to take pleasure in the sensory details within the tea room (**the joy of little things**), and to be in a state of mindfulness in which one takes the inner cosmos of the tea room into one's mind (**being in the here and now**).

This all echoes what we found out about the ancient Japanese concept of *wa* in Chapter 2. *Wa* is a key to understanding how people can promote their own sense of *ikigai* while living in harmony with other people. As previously mentioned, the seventeen-article constitution authored by Prince Shōtoku in 604 famously declared that '*Wa* is to be valued.' Since then, *wa* has been one of the defining features of Japanese culture and one of the key ingredients of *ikigai*. Prince Shōtoku can be considered as one of the pioneers of *ikigai* in this context.

Living in harmony with other people and the environment is an essential element of *ikigai*. An experiment published by researchers at Massachusetts Institute of Technology suggests that social sensitivity is a determining factor in the performance of a team. Each person's *ikigai*, when implemented in harmony with other people, promotes creativity in the free exchange of ideas. By appreciating and respecting the individual characteristics of people around you, you can realize a 'golden triangle' of *ikigai*, flow and creativity.

When you are in a state of flow, in harmony with the different elements inside and outside yourself, you have the cognitive capacity to pay attention to the various subtle nuances that come your way. When you are emotionally disturbed, or strongly biased, you lose the mindfulness necessary to appreciate the all-too-important details of things that can tip the balance of life and work. You can pursue quality best only when you are in a state of flow, a fact that Akuto and Koshimizu know only too well.

The relentless pursuit of quality is evident also in Japanese bars, at the consumption end of whisky making. Est! is a legendary bar in Yushima, Tokyo. Its proprietor is Akio Watanabe, who has been tending the customers in this institution for nearly four decades. In my humble opinion, the best bars in the world are to be found in Japan. I know this may sound biased and ridiculous, but this is from the perspective of someone who grew up in Tokyo, and later came to travel around the world. I have been to a few bars in my life!

I had the fortune to visit Est! when I was a college student, just over the legal drinking age of twenty years old.

The moment I stepped into the bar, somewhat nervous, I was to learn of a whole new world. The inside of Est! is decorated with the general motifs of a Japanese bar, with a hint of Irish and Scottish culture. Bottles of whisky, rum, gin and other favourites line the shelves.

In Japan, a bar like Est! is sometimes called a 'shot bar'. It is difficult to describe the unique atmosphere of a shot bar to somebody who has not been to one. In terms of the elegance of its customers and the tranquillity of its ambience, a Japanese shot bar is like a wine bar. In terms of being upmarket, it may share some qualities with the American concept of a fern bar, but then the customers are not necessarily singles or yuppies, nor is there any emphasis on greenery in the interior. The Japanese shot bar is in fact a genre of its own. There's nothing quite like it in the world.

The elegance of Watanabe's cocktail-making, the tranquil atmosphere, the way Watanabe listens to and responds to his customers was all a wonderful inspiration to me. It sounds like a cliché, but I learnt many valuable lessons of life while sitting at the counter that evening, sipping whisky.

This is Watanabe's secret: the relentless pursuit of quality, commitment, the focus on the small things without thinking about recognition. For many years, Watanabe did not take any holidays, except for a week at New Year and another week in the middle of August. The rest of the time, Watanabe has been standing behind the bars of Est! seven days a week, all year around. He gives attention to every single drink that he serves in his bar, taking every drink very seriously. Although Est! is highly regarded by its clients, who include actors, editors, writers and university professors, Watanabe never sought social recognition. He is extremely shy of any press or media attention. Once, I learned, from the casual comments of a customer sitting next to me at Est!, that Watanabe, in his youth, once served cocktails to the legendary novelist Yukio Mishima. In the thirty years I have frequented that place, Watanabe has never told me about this remarkable encounter. He is that kind of guy.

Here's one last and remarkable example of people doing something without any prospect of recognition. The Japanese Imperial household historically has a strong cultural tradition. Science and the arts have been considered an important part of the Imperial patronage. Music is central to them. The musicians serving the Imperial Family have designated roles in the provision of the special music for the hundreds of ceremonies and rituals held in the Imperial Palace every year. These traditional forms of ancient Imperial court music and dance together are called *gagaku*. *Gagaku* has been played at court for more than a thousand years.

I once had a conversation with Hideki Togi, a famous court musician in the *gagaku* tradition. Togi is from the Togi family, involved in *gagaku* since the Nara period (710–794), that is, for more than 1,300 years. Togi told me that the court musicians play at many occasions, such as the 1,200-year anniversary of a particular emperor. When I asked who would listen to such music, he simply replied 'nobody'.

He continued: 'We play instruments, sing and dance, while no audience is present, within the great tranquillity of the Imperial Palace. We play music late into the night. Sometimes, we feel as if the spirits of the deceased emperors come down from heaven, stay for a while with us, enjoy the music and then go back.' Togi said all this as if there was nothing extraordinary in what he was saying. Apparently, for musicians of the *gagaku* tradition, playing in the absence of an audience has always been something that is taken for granted.

Togi's narrative is a very poetic and poignant description of the state of flow, **being in the here and now**. Once you achieve a state of blissful concentration, an audience is not necessary. You enjoy the here and now, and simply go on.

In life, we sometimes misplace priorities and significance. Too often, we do something for the sake of rewards. If the rewards are not forthcoming, we are disappointed, and lose interest and zeal in the work. That is simply the wrong approach. In general, there are delays between actions and rewards. Even if you finish a good work, rewards are not necessarily forthcoming: reception and recognition occur in a stochastic way, depending on many parameters out of one's control. If you can make the process of making the effort your primary source of happiness, then you have succeeded in the most important challenge of your life.

So make music, even when nobody is listening. Draw a picture, when nobody is watching. Write a short story that no one will read. The inner joys and satisfaction will be more than enough to make you carry on with your life. If you have succeeded in doing so, then you have made yourself a master of **being in the here and now**.

CHAPTER 6

Ikigai and sustainability

Crucially, the Japanese conception of *ikigai* has always been one of reservation and self-restraint, where harmony with others is considered to be of primary importance. In a world where economic asymmetries have led to a widespread social unrest, Japan has traditionally remained a nation of modest means, despite its economic success in the past. For a long time, a majority of Japanese perceived themselves as belonging to the middle class. In recent years, with the slowdown of economic growth and aging of the population, there has been a growing awareness that economic asymmetry is increasing, and several metrics are consistent with that perception. However, extravagant spending by the rich or displays of exhibitionism by the famous are relatively rare in Japan, at least in perception. Japan has only a subdued celebrity culture. There are no Justin Biebers or Paris Hiltons, although Japan does have its share of celebrities on a diminished scale.

Curbing individual desires and ambitions might have negative side effects. Compared to the global success of such companies as Google, Facebook, and Apple, startups in Japan in recent years have had a relatively small impact. Maybe the Japanese spectrum of success and glamour is too narrow to accommodate true game changers on a global scale.

Closely connected to the subdued expression of individual freedom and success, to reservation and self-restraint, is one of Japan's most unique values: sustainability. The pursuit of individual desires is more often than not balanced with the sustainability of society and environment. After all, without a robust and healthy society and environment, you cannot pursue your goals, and aim to achieve your ambitions.

As we have seen earlier, on an individual level, *ikigai* is a motivational structure to keep you going, to help you get up in the morning and start doing chores. In Japanese culture, in addition, *ikigai* has much to do with being in harmony with the environment, with people around you and with society at large, without which sustainability is impossible. The third pillar of *ikigai*, **harmony and sustainability**, is perhaps the most important and uniquely developed ethos of the Japanese mindset.

Let us consider the Japanese relationship with nature. The Japanese have made the restraint of individual wants into an art form of modesty, austere aesthetics and elegant sufficiency. In Japanese idealism, there is an abundance of understated beauty, *wabi sabi*. The smooth untreated wood of a sushi counter is a quintessential example. The fragrant *hinoki* wood used in baths, combined with the peeled skins of *yuzu* orange fruit, is another one – and a heavenly one at that. The purpose of such a bath is not just to be clean, but to relax. Bathing outdoors in nature is quite popular, especially at *onsen* (hot springs). In urban areas, bringing nature indoors to fill the interior with simple luxury and comfort is very common. You will often find paintings of Mt Fuji on the walls of *sento* (public baths), for example – a very popular artistic trick.

Forest breathing and mountain climbing are popular hobbies in Japan, showing the respect and affection for nature felt by the Japanese. The design of the Japanese garden is crafted to be aesthetically pleasing, designed to grow into different scenes depending on the season.

Japan is a nation of sustainability. Sustainability applies not only to man's relation to nature, but also to the modes of individual activities within a social context. You should show adequate consideration for other people, and be mindful of the impact your actions might have on society at large. Ideally, every social activity should be sustainable. It is the Japanese spirit to pursue something in a subdued but sustained manner, rather than, in flamboyant fashion, seek short-lived satisfaction of momentary needs. As a consequence, when something is started in earnest in Japan, it is likely that it will be preserved in motion for a *very* long time.

The Japanese Emperor is the oldest hereditary monarch in the world. The current Emperor Akihito, whose reign began on 7 January 1989, is the 125th in the line. Many cultural institutions have been handed down over the centuries. *Noh* (a classical Japanese musical drama), *kabuki* (a classical Japanese dance-drama) and other forms of performing arts have been practised over generations. But there are many other old families in Japan, carrying the torch for different aspects of cultural and economic traditions.

The word 'family business' has a serious and historical significance in Japan. Many families are known to be involved in a particular field of cultural and economic activity, extending over centuries. The Ikenobo family in Kyoto has been dedicated to the art of *ikebana* (flower arrangement) since 1462 at the latest, according to a historic document. The Sen families, also in Kyoto, have been keeping the culture of the tea ceremony active for more than 400 years since the death of the founding father Sen no Rikyū in 1591. There are three Sen families, with tens of thousands of disciples practising the tea ceremony all over Japan and abroad. Toraya, a maker of traditional Japanese sweets operated by the Kurokawa family, has been in business for nearly 500 years. Kongō Gumi, founded in the year 578 by three carpenters, specializes in the construction and maintenance of temples, and is the world's oldest company currently in operation, with the Kongō family still at the helm.

*

Japanese culture abounds with memes and institutions implementing *ikigai* as an engine for sustainability. In order to understand how the Japanese perceive *ikigai*, one needs to understand the anatomy of sustainability, Japanese style. And this is very apparent at the Ise Shrine.

In a deep and vast forest spreading over 5,500 hectares in the Mie prefecture of western Japan lies one of the most important institutions of Japan's indigenous Shinto religion, the Ise Shrine. The Ise Shrine is considered to be the most sacred of Japanese Shinto shrines, and is dedicated to the sun goddess Amaterasu. In the Japanese legend, the Imperial family is descended from Amaterasu. The Ise Shrine has thus been closely associated with the Imperial House of Japan. The role of the chief priest of the shrine has been traditionally performed by members of the Imperial Family. It is so important that world leaders who attended the Ise-Shima G7 summit in 2016 visited the shrine.

The Ise Shrine is believed to house the sacred mirror (*Yata no Kagami*), one of the Three Sacred Treasures of the Imperial household, together with the sword (*Kusanagi*) and jewel (*Yasaka no Magatama*). A *magatama* is a jewel indigenous to

Japan, and is made of jade and shaped in a form similar to the human foetus. At the time of the Ascending to the Throne of a new Emperor, the Three Sacred Treasures are transferred as the symbol of the dignity and authority of the Imperial household. The physical presence of the Three Sacred Treasures has never been confirmed, as nobody (except the Emperor, perhaps) has actually seen these artifacts.

The religious attitude of the modern Japanese is a secular one. Many Japanese visit the Ise Shrine for worship, but it does not necessarily mean that they are deep believers of the Shinto doctrines, or even know the particulars of the belief system. Most Japanese regard a visit to the Ise Shrine as a cultural experience. Shinto itself is not a religion with strict rules and regulations. Independent of the religious context, the tranquillity of the deep forest and the serene beauty of the buildings of the Ise Shrine are inspirational, resonating with contemporary philosophies of the relationship between man and nature.

One of the most remarkable aspects of the Ise Shrine, and more relevant to our search for *ikigai* perhaps, is the periodic rebuilding of the shrine. There are two alternative sites for the Inner and Outer shrines of Ise. Every twenty years, the shrine building is carefully dismantled, and a new building of exactly the same structure is built on a new site, using newly obtained wood. The current buildings date from the year 2013. The next rebuilding will take place in the year 2033. Records suggest that this rebuilding process every two decades has been going on for the last 1,200 years, with occasional irregularities due to battles and social turmoil.

In order to sustain the exact rebuilding of the shrines, a number of careful considerations and preparations must be put in place. For example, the *hinoki* (Japanese cypress) tree must be grown many decades in advance to be used as logs in the shrine buildings. For that purpose, the Ise Shrine has reserves of *hinoki* trees all over the nation. Some of the logs used for the Ise Shrine must be of a certain size, a role fulfilled only by *hinoki* trees more than 200 years old.

There are special carpentry techniques used for the Ise Shrine. For example, the shrine buildings are constructed without using a single nail. The support and training of skilled carpenters dedicated to the shrine building is an essential part of the sustainability of the Ise Shrine. One theory has it that the rebuilding of the shrine every twenty years was designed to transmit the techniques and experience of shrine building from one generation of carpenters to another.

The Ise Shrine is the pinnacle of the tens of thousands of shrines all over Japan. Although smaller in scale and modest in appearance, these local shrines are respected and preserved by people in the neighbourhood. At present, about a hundred Shinto priests and 500 general staff support the operations of the Ise Shrine. Then there are the people who support the shrine in indirect manners, for example, carpenters, craftsmen, merchants and forestry people. The organization and harmony (as per Prince Shōtoku's *wa*) of these people who support the shrine is another important aspect of this venerable tradition of sustainability.

There was an undoubted genius in the conception and design of the Ise Shrine. Its buildings are exquisite and beautiful. A famous Buddhist priest, Saigyō (1118–1190), on his visit to the Ise Shrine, wrote a traditional *waka* poem which could be translated as, 'I don't know what resides here, but my soul sheds tears touching its divine serenity.'

Conception and design is one thing; maintenance of the

original setting over hundreds of years is quite another. Times are always changing. Governments come and go. People with varied abilities and personal traits will have been involved in its operation. It is simply a miracle that the Ise Shrine has been kept in pristine condition for over a thousand years.

Importantly, the Ise Shrine could not depend on the luxury of an excellent staff supporting its operation. To be sure, the shrine staff have a splendid reputation for reliability and ingenuity. I personally came to know a few of them, and they are truly model, conscientious workers, exhibiting aptitude. However, that is not the point. But for a built-in and assured mechanism to keep its operation going, the Ise Shrine could not have been kept going for more than a millennium.

For example, if you imagine how Apple would be operating for 1,000 years after Steve Jobs' death, you might start to appreciate the difficulty of the task. Similarly, the internet has surely changed the world, but nobody knows if it is sustainable for the next decades, let alone for hundreds of years. Hackers, frauds, trolls and information floods are just a few examples of concerns about the internet. The proliferation of fake news in the social media is putting the democratic system in jeopardy. There are in addition genuine worries about the increasingly savage race to lure people's attention and engagement time. We all know how various internet services, for example, Facebook, Twitter, Snapchat, Instagram, are shredding our waking hours into a random agglomeration of short attention spans.

How can an individual realize sustainability in life through *ikigai*, given his or her unique personality traits, in a world increasingly obsessed with innovations? The excellent track record of the Ise Shrine should be studied as a model for the realization of sustainability. Clearly, harmony is the key to sustainability. The reservation and humbleness of the Ise Shrine staff, against the backdrop of the excellent job they and their predecessors have done over so many years, make the Ise Shrine the apotheosis of **harmony and sustainability**, the third pillar of *ikigai*.

There is another shrine in the heart of Tokyo, which provides another unique case for sustainability. The Meiji Shrine, founded in 1920, is dedicated to Emperor Meiji

(1852–1912), who played a pivotal role in the modernization of Japan. It is a popular site for visitors from abroad. The display of *sake* barrels dedicated to the shrine is particularly popular, with people taking selfies in front of the colourful collection. People hang *ema* (wooden plaques) near the main shrine building, on which they have written their wishes. Reflecting the international popularity of the shrine, writings are found in various languages, expressing wishes concerning good health, happiness, academic achievement, and success in business.

Located in the heart of Tokyo, the shrine buildings are embedded in a deep forest, encompassing seventy hectares. Strolling through the forest on the way to the shrine is a popular activity for the Tokyoites and visitors. You can rest for tea or have various meals in the restaurants in the tranquil setting of the forest.

There is a colony of goshawks nesting in the Meiji Shrine grounds, symbolizing the richness of this huge forest in the centre of Tokyo. There are many rare species found in the Meiji Shrine forest. Walking through it, you have a feeling that you're breathing in a natural environment that has been here for a long time. In fact, the forest is artificial in its origin, conceived, planned and then executed by botanists, notably Seiroku Honda, Takanori Hongo, and Keiji Uehara.

At the time the Meiji Shrine was conceived, the site was a treeless barren land. The three botanists put a careful consideration into the selection of tree species to be planted. Based on their knowledge of ecological succession and how the species structure of a forest changes over time, they designed and foresaw how the community of trees would develop until it peaked and reached a steady state. Responding to the announcement of the plans, 120,000 trees of 365 species were donated by people from all over Japan, to commemorate and pay respects to the late Emperor, and mark the end of an era.

Today, almost one hundred years later, the results are tranquil natural surroundings in which one can relax and spend a meditative time.

What Honda, Hongo, Uehara and others did towards the founding of the Meiji Shrine forest was clearly a work of great ingenuity. Preservation of the forest then requires another tranche of work, which is equally important. Because the

Meiji Shrine forest is considered a sacred area, people are not allowed to wander into it, except on designated paths. Every morning, staff can be observed sweeping the path leading to the shrine buildings, removing fallen leaves with great care and elegance, a sight which gives much pleasure and inspiration to the onlookers. The staff then put the fallen leaves carefully back on the ground around the tree roots, rather than discarding them, thus replenishing precious nutrition for the forest. Over time, the leaves are decomposed by fungi and turn back to earth, contributing to the next generations of plants and leaves. This respect for the sanctuary has certainly helped preserve the goshawk colony that nests in the forest.

The Ise and Meiji shrines were clearly great instances of innovation, at the time of their conception. They are also models of sustainability. The Ise Shrine has maintained its rebuilding cycle for well over 1,000 years. The Meiji Shrine has been around for a hundred years, and it is not difficult to imagine it being kept in its current condition for hundreds of years to come.

Our *ikigai* would not be sustainable if we failed to

appreciate the efforts of the common people. In Japanese philosophy, what appears to be ordinary and mediocre is not necessarily ordinary or mediocre at all. The Japanese culture thrives because of the most simple and humble tasks – often taking them to a level of perfection. Without such a philosophy of life, many things, from the rebuilding of the Ise Shrine to the conception and maintenance of the Meiji Shrine forest, or the running of Shinkansen trains and wonderful food at sushi restaurants, would not be sustainable.

Needless to say, a value system centred on just the top few cannot be sustained, because somebody has got to be the underdog, in order for someone to be at the top. In today's world, where humans are increasingly forced to compete in a global context, we need to consider the implications and repercussions of this obsession with winning the competition. A mindset with the drive to win can lead to great innovations. The same mindset can also lead to excessive stress and instability, both for individuals and society.

The problem is, it is in man's nature to think in terms of hierarchies of winners and losers, leaders and followers, superiors and subordinates. That is why we have made progress thus far as a species, and that is why we might someday race to our own destruction. Studying *ikigai* in the context of restrained and moderate expression of the self, while considering the organic system that one finds oneself in, might well contribute to a sustainable way of living.

Such a line of thought is clearly related to the traditional concept of *wa*. Modulating one's desires and wants in harmony with the environment will also reduce unnecessary conflicts. In other words, *ikigai* is for peace!

Sustainability is an art of life, requiring ingenuity and skilfulness. A man is like a forest, individual yet connected and dependent on others for growth. The fact that someone has lived for a long time is quite an achievement, in the ups and downs of this often unpredictable world. After all, in the long process of life, you sometimes stumble and fall. Even at those times, you can have *ikigai*, even when you are on a losing streak. *Ikigai*, in a nutshell, is literally from the cradle to the grave, *no matter what happens in your life*.

So imagine you're in a tranquil forest. And take a deep

breath. And then consider what it would take to sustain that forest.

Whenever I visit the Meiji Shrine forest, I hearken to the beautiful murmurs of sustainability. *Ikigai* is small-scale, patient, mundane and long-sighted.

CHAPTER 7

Finding your purpose in life

As we have seen, *ikigai* is about the sustainability of life. Unexpectedly, in Japan the world of sumo is one of the hidden treasure troves of sustainability of life.

Sumo is a traditional form of wrestling that has a history dating back to antiquity. The professional sumo came into being in the early years of the *Edo* era, in the seventeenth century.

In the West, there is a prevalent (mis)conception of the sumo as a pushing and punching battle between two naked fat men with funny hairdos, wearing strange belts around their waists. That image is often a comical and (perhaps) derogatory one. There is naturally more depth to this ancient athletic activity. Otherwise, intelligent and sophisticated people would not go crazy over sumo as a spectator sport, let alone devote a whole career to it as athletes, as is the case.

Fortunately, as sumo gets internationally more popular, and with an increasing number of tourists from abroad visiting to see sumo wrestlers in action, the subtleties accompanying sumo wrestling are gradually beginning to be appreciated by a wider international audience.

The Grand Sumo Tournaments are held six times each year, three times at the Sumo Hall (*Ryōgoku Kokugikan*) in Tokyo and once each in Osaka, Nagoya and Fukuoka. A Grand Sumo Tournament runs for fifteen days, starting and ending on a Sunday. There is a strict ranking system of Sumo wrestlers, with *yokozuna* (grand champion) at the top. The aim and dream of every sumo wrestler is to climb up the ladder, although, needless to say, very few make it to *yokozuna*. One of the earliest *yokozuna*s whose records survive was Tanikaze, who was active as a sumo wrestler from 1789. Tanikaze had an incredible winning rate of 94.9%, second only to Umegatani, who had a winning rate of 95.1% (oh, yes, the Japanese did keep a detailed record of the sumo bouts even in those times). Tanikaze was active until 1795, when a sudden death from flu ended his incredible career. Many regard Tanikaze as one of the greatest (or, arguably, *the* greatest) *yokozuna* in the history of sumo.

Over a period of about 300 years, there have been 72 *yokozunas*, with four of them active at the time of writing. In 1993, Akebono, from Hawaii, USA, became the first *yokozuna* born abroad. He was the 64th *yokozuna* in history. Since the pioneering feat of Akebono, there have been five *yokozunas* from abroad, including the great Hakuhō from Mongolia, who holds, at the time of writing, the record of 38 championship wins in the Grand Tournaments.

There are six ranked divisions in the hierarchy of sumo wrestlers. A sumo wrestler belonging to the top two divisions is called a *sekitori*. Approximately only one in ten sumo wrestlers makes it to *sekitori*. Typically, there are about seventy *sekitori* wrestlers, while there are around 700 sumo wrestlers in total at any given time.

There is a huge world of difference between a *sekitori* and lower-ranked wrestlers. Not only do the lower-ranked wrestlers compete as fighters, but also they have to perform functions as assistants to the higher ranked *sekitori* wrestlers.

The assistants carry the *sekitori*'s clothes and belongings, while the *sekitori* himself goes empty-handed. Out of the ring, the fashion statement of a *sekitori* is that of *nonchalant cool*. He needs to appear to be street-smart, taking it easy. It will never do for a *sekitori* to sweat carrying heavy luggage. The younger sumo wrestlers carry that weight, while doing other odd jobs as well. A *sekitori* is allowed to wear a proper kimono, while the non-*sekitori* wrestlers are only allowed to wear *yukata*, a simple robe typically worn after one has taken a bath. It is then no wonder that every sumo wrestler aspires to be a *sekitori*.

Based on the performance of the tournaments, the sumo wrestlers get promoted or demoted. If you have more wins, you get a promotion. Otherwise you are demoted. The arithmetic of sumo wrestling is that simple. It is a classic zero-sum game situation. The more wins you have, the fewer wins other sumo wrestlers enjoy. Sumo, in essence, is where someone's success and promotion directly translates into the failure and demotion of someone else. The world of sumo is over-crowded; you need literally to push other wrestlers out of the ring to get promoted.

If you stay in the lower ranks, the economic reward you receive is minimal. Your food and bed will be guaranteed as long as you stay in the *heya* (training stable) where, typically, non-*sekitori* wrestlers sleep together in a large room. However, marrying and supporting a family is out of the question as the life of a non-*sekitori* gets tough with age. Success as a sumo wrestler might be one of the sweetest of Japanese dreams; the problem is that with the dream comes a high probability of failure. Nine out of ten, to be precise.

One of the training stables, Arashio stable, has special information on its website regarding the potential career choices of sumo wrestlers. After stating drily that only one in ten wrestlers makes it to *sekitori*, it offers three career choices, meant for someone who has spent five years training as a sumo wrestler:

(1) One may choose to carry on as a sumo wrestler. In that case, after a congratulatory ceremony commemorating the efforts over five years, he will be encouraged to continue.

(2) One may be undecided, feeling inclined to continue

as a sumo wrestler, while acknowledging the need to consider a second career. In that case, the stable will offer a year's consideration period, in which the stable master weighs up various possibilities, while the wrestler continues his efforts in the stable. After one year, the wrestler can make a decision about his future.

(3) One may feel that he has tried enough as a sumo wrestler, and want to enter a new stage in life. In that case, the stable master, together with the supporters of the stable, will seek job opportunities. In the process of the job search, the retired wrestler will be allowed to keep living in the stable quarters for a period of up to one year, with food and lodging provided.

The website then proudly states: 'When you consider the strenuous effort one must make to stay in a sumo stable, the retired wrestler will have the character and resources fit to start a successful second career.'

Sumo wrestlers can expect to have many second career jobs, sometimes helped by people who traditionally support them (collectively called *tanimachi*, after an area in Osaka from where such well-to-do supporters originated). For example, retired sumo wrestlers often open certain types of restaurant offering *chanko*, a special type of dish that sumo wrestlers eat in the training stable to help build up their body. A particularly famous dish is *chanko nabe* (*chanko* stew), where various nutritious ingredients, for example, meat, fish and vegetables, are cooked in a tasty soup. Contrary to popular belief, eating *chanko* in modest quantities does not lead to obesity. Many former sumo wrestlers have opened *chanko* restaurants inside and outside Tokyo, with varying degrees of success. The *tanimachi* sponsors typically provide the capital money to start the business, and frequent the restaurant as regular customers. There are other jobs offered to a retired wrestler, since the general perception is that a person who has endured the arduous training schemes of a sumo *heya* is ready to make his way in other fields of life as well. Examples of post-sumo careers include chiropractor, corporate worker, the construction business, hotel manager, sports instructor and even aeroplane pilot.

Financially speaking, therefore, it makes sense to give it

up and retire into a potentially lucrative post-sumo career, with the possibility of supporting a family. However, many sumo wrestlers who do not make it to *sekitori* carry on with their career, even if that means living on a minimum wage and having to carry out many strenuous chores as assistants.

The most senior sumo wrestler as of June 2017, Hanakaze, is forty-six years old. Hanakaze has a height of 182cm (5.97 feet) and a weight of 109kg (240 pounds). Hanakaze has been a wrestler for more than thirty-one years, fighting in 186 Grand Tournaments with a mediocre but not disastrous performance (605 wins and 670 losses). The highest rank Hanakaze has ever achieved was two divisions below the *sekitori*. Currently, Hanakaze is in the second lowest rank. Given his age and track record, it is not likely that Hanakaze will ever make it to *sekitori*. In an age-conscious nation such as Japan, and in a sport where the possibility of success decreases rapidly with age, the fact that Hanakaze keeps going despite his age is regarded as courageous.

Hanakaze has had a relatively respectable performance record. Hattorizakura has not been so lucky. Hattorizakura is currently eighteen years old, with a height of 180cm (5.9 feet) and a weight of 68kg (150 pounds). Hattorizakura has fought in eleven Grand Tournaments, with the performance of 1 win and 68 losses. Hattorizakura currently holds the record for consecutive losses as professional sumo wrestler. He drew media attention when in one bout, he was so afraid of his opponent Kinjo, who had the reputation of using hard punches, that he appeared deliberately to trip and fall to the ground, a movement that is immediately considered to signal a loss in sumo, of course. The fact that Hattorizakura looked so young and naive, and yet was a professional sumo wrestler all the same, stimulated people's imagination. Hattorizakura became a paradoxical star overnight. Needless to say, with his very poor performance, he has consistently stayed in the lowest division.

It is anybody's guess how long Hattorizakura will be able to (and willing to) continue as a professional sumo wrestler. He may give up one of these days, concluding that he is not fit for the sport. Otherwise, it is entirely possible that Hattorizakura will keep going for the next thirty years like Hanakaze. There is no rule in professional sumo that says you are asked to leave because of your performance record, no matter how poor it may be. It is up to each wrestler to decide whether he would like to stay in the competition, even when there is apparently no hope of promotion.

Why do sumo wrestlers like Hanakaze or Hattorizakura keep going when their performances are disappointing? Why do they prefer to stay in the world of a sport which does not treat them kindly? In other words, what are the low-performing wrestlers' *ikigai*? Well, as a sumo fan myself, I have an answer, or at least a hypothesis. It is all because of the magic of sumo. You will understand the magic if you ever step into the Sumo Hall in Tokyo, when the Grand Tournament is held. Once you become addicted to the world of sumo, you don't want to leave it so easily. It makes psychological sense to make small personal sacrifices, to stay within the wondrous kingdom.

On the one hand sumo is a serious full-contact sport. You need to train yourself to the extreme limit. You have to overcome your fears and crash into your opponent at full speed, a lesson the young Hattorizakura has yet to learn. On the other hand, sumo is so very rich in cultural tradition. A novice going to the Sumo Hall is amazed by the complexity and richness of the lengthy preparations leading up to a bout of wrestling. The bout itself ends in an average of just about ten seconds, and rarely extends over a minute. The vast majority of time at the Sumo Hall is spent in appreciating the subtle poetry of the sumo wrestlers' actions, the dignity of *gyoji* (judges), and the choreographed movements of *yobidashi* (ushers), who invite sumo wrestlers onto the ring by calling out their names in a ceremonial style. It is the combination of the no-nonsense crush of bone against bone and the elegance of ritual that is intoxicating.

Satonofuji, a sumo wrestler who is thirty-nine at the time of writing, has had a respectable if not remarkable career as a fighter. He has gone through 127 Grand Tournaments, with 429 wins and 434 losses. Satonofuji has a height of 171cm (5.61 feet) and a weight of 111kg (245 pounds), a small physique for a sumo wrestler. The highest rank Satonofuji has achieved is just below the *sekitori* threshold. Currently he is at the second lowest rank. Despite his modest performance, every sumo lover knows Satonofuji's name and his well-built but compact upper body. All because Satonofuji performs the *yumitori-shiki* (bow twirling) ceremony at the very end of a day's bouts during the Grand Tournament.

In the tradition of sumo, the bow twirling ceremony is performed by a sumo wrestler from the same training stable as a *yokozuna*. Satonofuji comes from the Isegahama stable, the same stable as the 70th *yokozuna* Harumafuji, who is from Mongolia. After the winner of the final bout (usually involving a *yokozuna*) is announced, the spectators are kindly requested to stay in their seats, to observe the bow twirling ceremony. Satonofuji holds and twirls the bow of about two metres in length with incredible speed and precision, to the applause of the audience. Finally, as Satonofuji bows and leaves the ring, a day's activities at the Sumo Hall comes to a close. Observing Satonofuji perform the bow twirling ceremony, you realize that this is perhaps his greatest *ikigai*.

There is a jinx in sumo that a wrestler who performs the bow twirling cannot make it to the *sekitori*, a curse broken only by a few sumo wrestlers so far.

However, for those who admire the sheer dexterity and

elegance of bow twirling by Satonofuji, his performance in the bouts hardly matters. Rather, it is felt that Satonofuji has found a niche in the world of sumo, a role that he can fulfil with joy and pride, a part of the rich set of traditions that is sumo. It is fitting that Satonofuji finds personal pleasure and joy as he twirls the bow, for the ceremony originated as a dance of gratitude by the sumo wrestler who wins the last bout of the day. (A sumo wrestler, even after winning a crucial bout, does not express his joy himself, out of respect for the opponent, who would be disappointed by the loss.) Even though Satonofuji is unlikely to be promoted any further, he will be very happy, until the end of his career as a sumo wrestler, to fulfil his role as the bow twirler.

Sumo is an ecological system where you can keep being an active player, as long as you find some niches, even if you keep losing in the bouts. Hanakaze, Hattorizakura and Satonofuji are all unsung heroes, having reasons to be proud in their own right, even though their performances are not good enough for them to be promoted to *sekitori*.

Sumo provides an inspirational case for the diversity and

robustness of *ikigai*. It tells a story of how one can find one's *ikigai* even in a world where the rules describing wins and losses are extremely strict. In many areas of human activity, value systems used to measure one's performances are subtle and open to alternative interpretations, so that one can even have self-delusions, and feel that one is doing alright. Sumo wrestlers cannot enjoy that kind of ambiguity or self-delusion. That does not, however, prevent them from having a sense of *ikigai*.

The *ikigai* of being a sumo wrestler depends on many things. Actually, all Five Pillars of *ikigai* are involved, just as in the tea ceremony. **Starting small** helps, as the training of a sumo wrestler depends on very detailed body-building techniques, such as a particular way of carrying one's feet on the ring. **Releasing oneself** is necessary, when, as an assistant to an elder wrestler, one has to attend to the needs and desires of the person one respects and serves. **Harmony and sustainability** is the very essence of sumo as a traditional sport, where many rituals and customs are designed to sustain the rich ecological system. **Joy of small things** abounds in the world of sumo, from the taste of *chanko* dishes to the cheering by the fans. Many wrestlers testify that **being in the here and now** is absolutely necessary in preparing for and fighting in a bout, as only by being immersed in the present can one hope to sustain the state of mind for optimum performance.

All these finely connected pillars of *ikigai* support a sumo wrestler, if he is not very successful, or even if he is not at all successful, in fighting the bouts. The *ikigai* in the world of sumo is very democratic, even if the sport itself is pretty cut-throat and unforgiving.

I am not claiming here that sumo is unique in the democratic provision of *ikigai* to everybody. A similar democratic *ikigai* structure can be found in, for example, the world of classical ballet.

As the host of a radio programme, I once had the opportunity to interview Manuel Legris, the French ballet dancer who was *Étoile* (principal dancer) at the Paris Opéra Ballet for twenty-three years. When Legris was just twenty-one years old, the legendary ballet dancer Rudolf Nureyev promoted him to *Étoile,* after seeing his performance as the lead role of Jean de Brienne in the ballet *Raymonda*. After that,

Legris performed various roles in such cities as Paris, Stuttgart, Vienna, New York and Tokyo. He is now the artistic director at Vienna State Ballet.

During the interview, Legris discussed the role of the *corps de ballet*, the dancers who dance as a group in a ballet performance, excellent dancers in their own right. It is extremely difficult to be selected for the *corps de ballet* at such prestigious ballet companies as the Paris Opéra Ballet, quite apart from making it to the rank of principal dancer. Legris said, with a strong conviction, that the role of *corps de ballet* is very important, as it constitutes an integral part of the spectacle on stage. In fact, the dancers in the back rows have the most important roles, with heavy demands on their skills. Legris then added that every principal dancer is naturally sympathetic to members of the *corps de ballet*, as he or she will have been a member of it at some stage in his or her career.

The roles played by dancers in the *corps de ballet* might be artistically important, but they are not necessarily well rewarded. A 2011 *New York Times* article reported that 'the Chicago-based Joffrey Ballet and the Boston Ballet paid their dancers average salaries of $829 and $1,204 per week, respectively, over 38-week seasons. The Houston Ballet paid its dancers $1,036 per week over 44 weeks.' These wages, while quite respectable, do not compare with the rewards that principal dancers receive. Thus, wage-wise, there may be a similar career structure and challenges in the world of ballet dancers as with sumo wrestlers.

As so often in life, you need to accept what you're given, and then rise to the situation. Biologically speaking, finding *ikigai* in an environment, or, for that matter, in *any* environment, could be regarded as a form of adaptation, especially in the context of mental fitness. In any given environment, it is in principle possible to have *ikigai*, the reason for living, no matter what one's performances might be.

It is not only winners that have *ikigai*. Winners and losers can have *ikigai* on an equal footing, in the great coordinated dance that is life. Seen from the inner perspective of *ikigai*, the border between winner and losers gradually melts. Ultimately there is no difference between winners and losers. It is all about being human.

In the minds of many Japanese, the song of *ikigai* is

sung for the underdogs, or at least for ordinary people from all walks of life. You don't have to be a top performer to have *ikigai*. Actually, *ikigai* can be found at every level of the hierarchy of competitive standing. *Ikigai* is a universal commodity, to be handed out to everyone with an eye for it.

In order to have *ikigai*, you need to go beyond the stereotypes and listen to your inner voice. It will appear that you can find your *ikigai* even when the political system of your home country is far from perfect, to say the least.

In the hermit state of North Korea, 'mass games' are a staple of everyday life. They were originally conceived in Germany and then developed in Japan as a school gymnastics activity. Today the genre is regularly and conspicuously performed in North Korea, with a high degree of sophistication.

The documentary film *A state of mind* (2004) by British film director Daniel Gordon follows the experience of two North Korean young female gymnasts and their families in the course of participation in the 2003 Pyongyang mass games. Such games have been performed in the country since 1946. Up to 80,000 gymnasts perform in a vast floor display. Through coordinated efforts, they create the biggest moving picture in the world.

Mass games is a format in which there is an organized subordination of an individual's desires to the needs of the collective. The participants train for a long period of time, for a minimum of two hours per day, to cultivate the group mentality. Although the sight of mass games might give an impression of mindless collectivism, the participants of the mass games are, needless to say, individuals with their own desires and dreams.

In *A State of Mind*, one of the young female gymnasts who participates eagerly in the mass games recalls her excitement as she performed before the 'General' (the late Kim Jong-il, son of Kim Il-sung, the founder of North Korea and father of Kim Jong-un, the current supreme leader of the hermit state). Her joys and ambitions are quite personal, albeit embedded in the social context of the state.

When watching *A State of Mind*, you realize that although the performance in the mass games itself might be collective and mechanical, the desires and joys a performer experiences during participation are very passionate and personal. Here's the great paradox of the relationship between an individual and the society, which a perspective from *ikigai* could clarify.

It is certainly possible to live in a totalitarian state and have *ikigai*. You can have an individual sense of *ikigai* even in a nation where freedom is limited. You can find *ikigai* independently of the particular environment you might find yourself in at a particular time.

Humans have the resourcefulness to find *ikigai* in any circumstances. Even in the Kafkaesque worlds depicted in *The Castle* or *The Trial*, the protagonists manage to have *ikigai*, actually quite a lot of it. The characters in both novels barely have breathing space to express their freedom. However, they have little joys to enable them to carry on with their lives. For example, in *The Castle*, the main character has a lot of success in finding lovers, even as he struggles to go through the maze of an oppressive bureaucratic system.

If we keep looking at the arts, you'll discover that you might even be able to find your *ikigai*, ironically, in successfully dropping an atomic bomb, which would lead to the end of the world. In *Dr. Strangelove or: How I Learned to Stop Worrying and Love the Bomb*, a 1964 film directed and co-written by the American film director Stanley Kubrick, Major Kong, commander on a B-52 bomber, becomes so obsessed with delivering the atomic bomb that he enters the bomb bay personally, and mends the electronic wiring. As the bomb is successfully dropped, Major Kong rides on it like a cowboy on a rodeo bull, giving a yell of joy, while bringing an end to human civilization.

Well, let's go back to the real world.

What have we learned? That *ikigai* is an adaptation to the environment, no matter what the nature of that environment might be. From sumo to classical ballet, people who find *ikigai* can find joys beyond the simplistic value of wins and losses. Having *ikigai* contributes towards making the very best of circumstances, which might otherwise be difficult – regardless of the fact they might be difficult.

You need to find your *ikigai* in the little things. You've got to start small. You need to be here and now. Most crucially, you cannot and should not blame the environment for a lack of *ikigai*. After all, it is up to you to find your own *ikigai*, in your own way.

In that respect, the famous Second World War slogan poster by the British government, 'Keep Calm and Carry On', could well be an ethos for *ikigai*. Who would have thought it?

CHAPTER 8

What doesn't kill you makes you stronger

One of the benefits of having *ikigai* is robustness and resilience – both strengths that are very necessary when tragedy occurs. To be resilient in one's life is important, especially given how increasingly unpredictable and even chaotic the world is becoming.

In 2012, I gave a talk at the TED conference in Long Beach California. The topic was the resilience of the Japanese people, one year after the Great Eastern Japan earthquake and tsunami of 2011 which took the lives of more than 15,000 people.

The very moment the earthquake hit, I was on a Tokyo subway. The tremor was like nothing I had experienced before, despite being from a nation frequently hit by earthquakes. The train stopped, and I walked the long way home.

On my smartphone, I watched in total disbelief the massive tsunami attacking the Tohoku area. It was a terrible experience.

I gave my whole heart to that TED talk. I used the footage of tsunami waves hitting the city of Kamaishi, waving a flag lent to me by a fisherman in the devastated city as a symbol of courage and hope. I talked about the Japanese spirit of resilience. Among Japanese fishermen, there is a saying, 'Under the board, there is hell.' Once Mother Nature rages, there is nothing you can do about it. Despite the risks, a fisherman ventures off into the ocean, to do his best to make a living. It was in that spirit, I argued, that people in the area hit by the earthquake and tsunami were bouncing back.

Japan is a nation which is prone to natural disasters. Over the years, the country has been struck by a series of catastrophes. Just like the fishermen after the earthquake and tsunami, the people of Japan have exhibited a great spirit of resilience after literally every disaster.

Volcanic eruptions are major causes of destruction for the nation. In 1792, Mt Unzen erupted, collapsing one of its lava domes, causing a megatsunami which claimed nearly 15,000 lives. The last eruption of Mt Fuji was in 1707, and it lasted for two weeks. Although there were no recorded casualties from the eruption, volcanic ash fell over a wide area, reaching Tokyo (called Edo at that time), and causing serious damage to agricultural land.

The year 1707 was an *annus horribilis* for Japan. Just forty-nine days prior to the eruption of Mt Fuji, a major earthquake and tsunami hit western Japan, resulting in nearly 20,000 deaths. The earthquake and the eruption of Mt Fuji are likely to have been causally connected. More recently, the Great Kanto earthquake of 1923, which hit the area round Tokyo, resulted in the deaths of more than 100,000 people. The experience of the quake provided a background story for the 2013 Hayao Miyazaki film *The Wind Rises*. Ise-wan typhoon, or Typhoon Vera in the year 1959, which made landfall near Nagoya, resulted in more than 5,000 casualties.

Given this kind of track record of natural disasters, it is difficult for the average Japanese not to have been exposed to the brutal forces of nature at some point in their lifetime.

In addition to natural disasters, there have been human ones, too. Japanese houses were traditionally built with wood. Before the arrival of modern fireproofing technology, these buildings burnt down easily. Consequently, there has been a series of major fires, bringing destruction and death on a large scale. The Great Fire of Meireki in 1657, which according to a widely known legend was caused by an incident involving a cursed kimono, spread to a wide area of Edo. Fuelled by strong wind, the fire ravaged for three days and destroyed 70 per cent of the capital, killing 100,000 people. The main tower of the Edo castle, where the Shogun resided, was burned down, and was never rebuilt during the Edo era which lasted until 1867.

In the bombings of Tokyo during the Second World War, great damage was inflicted on the capital. In particular, on the nights of 9 and 10 March, 1945, in what the Allied Forces called 'Operation Meetinghouse', hundreds of B-29 bombers dropped cluster bombs, releasing napalm-carrying incendiary bomblets. As a result, the traditional downtown area of Tokyo was totally destroyed, killing 100,000 people. This was particularly tragic, when you consider it was less than twenty-two years after the destruction caused by the Great Kanto earthquake of 1923, which left exactly the same area virtually annihilated.

Today, if you stand on a busy street in Tokyo, you would be amazed at finding no trace of the unimaginable damage once inflicted upon those areas. The areas affected by the bombing of Tokyo in 1945 today enjoy the same peace and prosperity as the rest of the capital. One can only hope that this will be so for the foreseeable future.

Where do the Japanese find the energy to carry on?

Some people might find sources and inspirations for resilience in social norms and ethics. Education and financial security play important roles too, as do family ties and friendships.

This message is taught at an early age in Japan. The *Weekly Shōnen Jump*, a manga magazine published by Shueisha, Tokyo, boasts a circulation of over 2 million copies. Over the years, the world's bestselling manga weekly has pledged three values to define the message of the works it carries: friendship, struggle, and victory. These three foundations of life were originally determined based on questionnaires presented to fourth and fifth graders at primary school. Japanese kids grow up with a keen awareness of the important values of life, where the various patterns of coping with hardships and overcoming them through collaboration with one's friends are fed into their brains through works of manga. This helps contribute to the fact that Japanese children have a clear sense of *ikigai* (friendship, struggle and victory in the case of *Weekly Shōnen Jump*) when they are still very young.

But it is clear that religion plays and has always played a fundamental part in the country's resilience. And it is a particular kind of religion.

Historically, the Japanese approach to religion has been epitomized by the idea of '8 million gods', where '8 million' stands for virtual infinity. The Japanese people have traditionally cherished the idea that there are infinitely more sources for religious meaning and values in life, as opposed to a single one representing the will of a deity.

There are worlds of differences between a single God who tells you what to do and how to live your life, and the Japanese conception of 8 million gods. The single God tells you what is good and bad, decides who goes to heaven or hell. In

Shinto, where you believe in 8 million gods, the belief process is more democratic. Shinto is constructed of small rituals, in which the mindfulness of nature and the environment is expressed. And rather than focusing on the afterlife, which is a big part of Christianity, the emphasis is more on the here and now, and how humans are part of a web of elements that make the world what it is. The Japanese believe that diverse elements, free from restrictions of strict religious doctrines, need to enter the practical and secular aspects of life, and the idea of 8 million gods is a kind of metaphor for such a philosophy.

It is important to acknowledge that there have been external influences along the way. The mindfulness embedded in the Japanese philosophy of life has been influenced by the Buddhist tradition of meditation, promoting long-term improvement and good behaviour. There is also a rather surprising link between *ikigai* and values described in *Ecclesiastes*, one of the twenty-four books of the Hebrew Bible, where life is viewed as fundamentally vain and futile. Because of this, *Ecclesiastes* recommends that we find pleasure in life's small rewards, as being something handed down by God,

which humans should receive with humble appreciation –
very in tune with the philosophy of *ikigai*.

There have also been impacts of Confucianism on Japanese culture, especially with regard to how one should behave in the secular sense, the relationship between the master and disciple and the respect you are supposed to show for your elders. The concept of changing the outside world by changing yourself, a point emphasized in the Japanese tradition of Zen, is a culmination of such multitudes of influences.

In the world, everything is connected, and no one is an island.

The Japanese take it for granted that everything religious is put in the secular, everyday context. Although most Japanese are not aware of the historical background behind this seemingly frivolous approach to religion, the idea of 8 million gods, in which the Japanese see deities in things surrounding them, from humans to animals and plants, from the mountains to small daily items, surely provides the underlying tone.

Japanese martial arts, be it a sumo bout or a judo match,

begin and end with a bow. As we have already seen, when a sumo wrestler wins a bout, he does not express his joys openly, out of respect for the defeated. The defeated wrestler, on the other hand, admits his defeat with grace. Every sumo or judo wrestler is a good loser by definition, at least ideally or on the surface. It is all about mutual respect. This is an example of taking pleasure and satisfaction in doing small things properly, for the greater good.

In the mind of the Japanese, the application of the philosophy of 8 million gods is not limited to humans, or, for that matter, living things. Lifeless items can treat humans favourably, as long as we pay due respect. However, if we treat them in a careless and heartless manner, they might harbour a grudge, and might strike back. A famous ancient Japanese scroll featuring a hundred monsters (*Hyakki Yagyō*) depicts some old household items (such as bowls, brooms and clothes) turning into monsters and parading the streets. It was believed back then that household items might become monsters after many years of use, especially if humans didn't treat them with due respect. Those household items which have turned into monsters are sometimes given the name '*tsukumokami*', or ninety-nine gods, where 'ninety-nine' (years) symbolically represents a long time. Thus, there are gods inside household items. That belief sets the unconscious undertone for many Japanese today.

The Japanese concept of god, as in 8 million gods, is different from the Western conception of God. When a Japanese says he or she believes that there is a god in a household item, what is implied is the necessity to pay due respect to that item, rather than saying that a god who created the whole universe is miraculously encapsulated in that small space.

Attitudes are reflected in people's actions. A person who believes that there is god inside an item will approach life differently from one who doesn't. The belief might manifest itself to varying degrees in day-to-day behaviour. There will be people who express their beliefs in a god of small things, while others might pay respect to and treat items around them carefully, without necessarily consciously believing that there are gods inside them. It is not uncommon to see baggage handlers and airport staff bow and wave goodbye to departing aeroplanes, a scene quite ordinary to many

Japanese but a source of inspiration and wonder for many people from abroad.

In the view of a typical Japanese, life is a balance of many small things, rather than something to be dictated down from a unifying doctrine. Although a flimsy attitude towards religion might raise eyebrows in some societies, for a Japanese it is quite natural to have a portfolio of religious motifs. From the Japanese viewpoint, religious themes are welcome, as long as they contribute to the multitude of a secular base for life.

The importance of secular values as opposed to strict religious value systems is an important aspect of the Japanese way of life, which has much to do with a robust construction of *ikigai*. The Japanese, even when they express allegiance to some religious organization, seldom do so with strictness, to the exclusion of other religions. It is not uncommon for a Japanese to visit the Shinto Shrine on New Year's Day, celebrate Christmas with a lover, get married in the Christian style and attend a Buddhist funeral. There isn't really an awareness of inconsistency. In recent years, for many Japanese, Christmas, Halloween and Easter are seen as festivities where you can go out on the street, shop and have a good time. In other words, the Japanese assimilate these religious traditions from abroad within the context of 8 million gods.

In the past, such a 'flexibility' has been criticized as a lack of 'true' religious belief. However, in the context of the contemporary world situation, where people from different religious backgrounds sometimes clash with tragic consequences, the apparently religiously frivolous Japanese mindset might be given the thumbs up. The pursuit of individual *ikigai* Japanese style, with a full spectrum of values, can be seen to contribute to a peace of mind in a world where extremisms tend to take hold.

That is not to say that Japan has been completely immune to religious conflicts. Throughout the history of Japan, there has been at times brutal oppression of religion, especially when perceived to be in conflict with secular values. In 1571, for example, in a series of events now called the Siege of Mount Hiei, the samurai warlord Nobunaga Oda (who killed himself in Honnō-ji temple, destroying the fourth starry bowl on the way, as described in Chapter 3) burned down hundreds of temples, massacring more than 20,000 monks and civilians. Some historians claim that this atrocity effectively curbed religious cults from having the power to overshadow the Japanese secular ways of living.

Christianity was brought to Japan by a number of missionaries, most notably Francis Xavier (1506–1552), who became the first missionary to reach Japan in 1549. In the beginning, the samurai warriors welcomed the newly arrived belief and culture, with its exotic flavour. There were even some high-profile cases in which samurai lords converted themselves to Christianity. After a honeymoon period, Hideyoshi Toyotomi, a powerful warlord, declared a ban on Christianity in 1587, and then again in 1596. The ban had many loose ends, and some missionaries continued their activities in Japan.

When given a choice between devout dedication to one principle and an array of ideologies, a typical Japanese would choose the latter. This has helped the nation to absorb many new things from abroad, as there is little taboo limiting the curiosity of people. On the other hand, looking at the balance of small things has made it difficult to stick to one principle. In the Martin Scorsese feature film *The Silence*, an adaptation of the masterpiece novel by Shūsaku Endō, the Jesuit priest, Father Rodrigues, who apostates under pressures from the Shogunate officials, likens Japan to a 'swamp', where nothing can take firm root. The priest goes on to say that even if Christianity appears to be believed, it is something different from the original, modified and digested in the Japanese way. In a land of 8 million gods, the Christian concept of God might have difficulty taking.

'Swamp' might sound derogatory, but in fact it is not necessarily so. The derogation is in the prejudice of the observer, not in the nature of the swamp itself. A swamp is a rich ecological system where many microorganisms thrive. Life on earth probably originated from an environment similar to a swamp. In our intestine, which in recent years has been shown to play an important role in our immune system, there is a rich ecosystem of microorganisms indispensable for the maintenance of our health.

One's *ikigai* is actually like a swamp, if there is enough diversity and depth to it. In short, there is a glory in the swamp. There might even be 8 million gods.

Ask yourself this: what are the small things in the swamp

of your mind that will carry you through a difficult patch? These are perhaps the elements you want to focus on and keep very present in your mind.

CHAPTER 9

Ikigai and happiness

There is a popular conception, justified to some extent, that the Japanese salaryman is a model of devotion and self-denial. The word *karoshi*, which literally means 'death from overwork', has entered the international lexicon. However, the old ethic of unquestioned devotion to one's company is becoming unacceptable, even in a country like Japan.

We all know intuitively that strict adherence to the work ethic demanded by an organization does not necessarily lead to happiness. In order to have a robust sense of *ikigai*, you need to keep a balance between work and life. New waves of alternative forms of *ikigai*, for example, salarymen quitting their companies and starting their own way of life, or househusbands doing the domestic chores for their working wives, have arrived in Japan. They reflect the global trend of working freelance. At the same time, there are some uniquely Japanese twists to these growing trends.

For example, *datsusara* is a phenomenon in which a salaried worker, usually employed in office work, decides to leave the safe but unexciting life as company employee to pursue their passions. Etymologically, *datsu* means 'to exit', whereas *sara* is an abbreviation for 'salarymen'. Sometimes, depending on the economic situation, you might be forced into *datsusara* after getting the boot. However, this has been relatively rare in Japan where, once employed, your job is usually secured until retirement. The forms *datsusara* may take are numerous: running a bar or a restaurant, becoming a farmer or an artist. A common characteristic is that these occupations are most often examples of extended *ikigai* – the former employee wishing to earn some kind of a living while doing something they feel passionate about, something they find interesting and fulfilling.

The ethos that you can have *ikigai* outside the context of your job resonates well with that of *datsusara*. Even the sumo wrestlers, who need to dedicate their lives to the punishing training of the sport, are known to have various hobbies, such as singing Karaoke or fishing, which will help them in any post-sumo careers.

Needless to say, the extracurricular activity as a source of joys of life is not a phenomenon limited to Japan.

In the legendary British comedy series *Father Ted*, each of the main characters has his or her own reason to live, apart from fulfilling their respective job descriptions. The now classic comedy depicts the lives of three Catholic priests and their housekeeper, living cosily together in a parochial house on the fictional Craggy Island. Father Ted Crilly is very keen on making money, gaining social recognition and has an eye on the fairer sex. Father Dougal McGuire tries to take it easy in general, while Father Jack Hackett just goes after 'drink'. Mrs Doyle is very fond of making tea, so much so that she stays up all night in the parlour, just in case someone would like a nice cup of tea in the middle of the night. The script, written by Graham Linehan and Arthur Mathews, depicts the haphazard adventures caused by the idiosyncracies of these main characters.

Although they don't put it in so many words, the favourite activities of the main characters of *Father Ted* contribute to their sense of *ikigai*. In one episode, Father Ted is addicted to smoking, Dougal to rollerskating and Jack to drink. They have a hard time giving up these habits, while they never think of leaving the priesthood, which does not interfere with their pursuit of their favourite pastimes anyway.

Although it is a work of fiction, the setup of *Father Ted* is instructive in demonstrating some aspects of what *ikigai* entails. First, *ikigai* does not have to be directly associated with one's professional life. For the three Catholic priests, the reasons for living have nothing to do with their obligations as priests (though, it is fair to say, they do not do any priestly things in the first place). Second, a reason for living could be something that appears to be strenuous and unnecessary from the viewpoint of others. Although making tea involves a lot of trouble, Mrs Doyle simply cannot stand the idea of being relieved of her task. In one episode, when Father Ted presents Mrs Doyle with a brand new tea maker, she secretly resents it, and sets out to destroy the expensive machine when nobody is around, so that she can continue to enjoy the misery of tea making.

Although the characters of *Father Ted* are larger than life, we can all sympathize with their personal *ikigai*, even if it is for comic effect.

The Japanese, as ever, have their own agenda when it comes to pastimes. Because employees in modern Japanese companies are often not fulfilled by the work they do, Japan is a country of hobbyists, engaged in pursuits unrelated to their day jobs. Enjoying hobbies in a big way is in a sense an exaggerated case of **joy of small things**. People enjoy a sense of achievement in seeing a task through to completion. To the extent that *ikigai* activity produces something of worth, it seems that the enjoyment of that end product is in the satisfaction of having done something — for example, eating your own home-grown vegetables. Satisfaction comes from creating something from start to finish, where people take pleasure and satisfaction in both the process and the result.

An incredible number of people are actively producing their own manga, selling them in the *comiket* (short for comic market) at weekends. In fact, participation in a *comiket* can be regarded as a prime example of *ikigai*.

Although *comiket* as a general noun could refer to countless similar meetings inside (and these days also outside)

Japan dedicated to the meetings of comic fans, the largest *comiket*, the *Comiket*, is held twice a year (in August and December) at the Tokyo Big Site, an exhibition hall complex in Tokyo's newly developing Odaiba area. Tokyo Big Site boasts a futuristic robot-like appearance and, as a venue for *Comiket*, has been a symbolic destination for devout comic fans. Starting from the humble first meeting in 1975 with just 600 attendees, the *Comiket* has now grown into a major fan and media event with 100,000s of participants each year. To date, *Comiket* is the largest meeting of such a kind in the world, followed by the San Diego Comic-Con International meeting, which attracted around 16,700 attendees in 2015. By comparison, the 2016 *Comiket* winter meeting attracted around 550,000 attendees.

Participants in *Comiket* sell *dojinshi*, which are self-published works of manga and related items. The sellers are called 'circles'. In a typical meeting, there will be around 35,000 circles. As the space is limited, there is a stringent selection and lottery process, determining which circles are permitted to participate. In a typical meeting, the acceptance rate is around 50 to 70 per cent.

A seller pays a fee of about 10,000 yen ($100), and is given an exhibition space of 90cm x 45cm. It may be a humble stall in size, but for hopeful sellers and eager buyers it is the stuff that dreams are made of. Although it does not happen often, a *Comiket* seller may find their way up to the competitive professional market. A rare and popular *dojinshi* work can fetch ten times or even a hundred times the original *Comiket* price on the auction sites. The majority of circles, however, are content with selling a modest number of *dojinshi* to the attendees. Some of the circles have a devout fan base, with the would-be buyers rushing to the stalls as the gates open in the morning.

The organization of *Comiket* is supported by amateur volunteers. In a typical meeting, around 3,000 volunteers work in an efficient collaboration. An NHK documentary broadcast in 2015 showed how the volunteers arrange around 6,000 tables used for sales stalls within an hour, in an impressive choreographic motion picture.

Apart from the *dojinshi* sales, a feature which has made *Comiket* conspicuous and famous is cosplay (costume play) activity, in which participants don costumes depicting famous anime or manga characters and pose for spontaneous photo sessions. The cosplayers come to Tokyo Big Site in their ordinary clothes (after all, it is not possible for characters from *Dragon Ball* or *Naruto* to be on an underground train without attracting embarrassing attention, even in Tokyo) and change into character outfits once they are in the safe and sympathetic haven of *Comiket*. In a typical meeting, it is estimated that there are approximately 27,000 cosplayers, which makes up about 5 per cent of all attendees.

The cosplayers make incredible efforts to transform themselves into characters of their fancy. Why would they do this? A girl featured in the NHK documentary testifies that she enjoys the transformation she experiences in the process of cosplay. Thus, a reserved working girl can become an object of attention and admiration to eager fans, once she completes the transformation into an anime character of her choice.

The *Comiket* is increasingly becoming an international event. In 2015, about 2 per cent of the visitors were from abroad. This figure is expected to increase in coming years. There are multilingual volunteers on site helping people from other countries. The *Comiket* website gives instructions in four languages (Japanese, English, Chinese, and Korean). International media such as CNN and the BBC have covered the event in the past. Time lapse video showing the incredibly disciplined and rational calm of the crowd waiting patiently to enter the *Comiket* exhibition hall has caused an international sensation.

Despite the increasingly global interest, there are many characteristics of *Comiket* which have remained largely Japanese in nature. A study of values and behavioural patterns exhibited by participants of *Comiket* reveals an interesting array of morals and standards that are reflected in the philosophy of *ikigai*.

The participants' incentives come mainly from the joy of doing the task itself, rather than financial reward or social recognition. It is certainly true that a successful cosplayer receives much attention during *Comiket*. That does not, however, automatically translate into a career or a financial windfall. A cosplayer, after enjoying fifteen minutes of fame at the *Comiket*, would not quit their day job.

Participation in the *Comiket* provides a sense of *ikigai* in a uniquely Japanese way. For example, there is no star system.

Attention and applause are given to each participant equally, even though, naturally, there are variations on the sales figures and fan base. There are no awards given out at the meetings, and each seller (circle) is treated in the same humble manner (with their 90cm x 45cm of promotion space).

The way the *Comiket* is organized suggests how *ikigai* can be associated with a general sense of happiness. Indeed, *ikigai* is closely related to our conception of happiness. We all want to be happy, and you would feel happier if you had some *ikigai*. How people perceive happiness is an interesting scientific question, as well as a matter of practical concern.

People tend to assume that there are some necessary conditions for happiness. In the hypothetical formula for happiness, one needs to possess, or have access to, several different elements, such as education, employment, a marital partner and money. In fact, scientific research suggests that there are few elements in human life which are absolutely necessary for someone to become happy. For example, contrary to popular belief, having a lot of money does not lead to happiness. You certainly need to have enough to live comfortably, but, beyond that, money cannot buy happiness.

Having children does not necessarily lead to more happiness. Marriage, social status, academic success – those elements of life which are often regarded as necessary to advance one's happiness actually have little to do with happiness *per se*.

Researchers have been investigating a phenomenon called 'focusing illusion'. People tend to regard certain things in life as necessary for happiness, while in fact they aren't. The term 'focusing illusion' comes from the idea that you can be focused on a particular aspect of life, so much so that you can believe that your whole happiness depends on it. Some have the focusing illusion on, say, marriage as a prerequisite condition for happiness. In that case, they will feel unhappy so long as they remain single. Some will complain that they cannot be happy because they don't have enough money, while others will be convinced they are unhappy because they don't have a proper job.

In having a focusing illusion, you create your own reason for feeling unhappy. If unhappiness is a vacuum in which the required element is absent, that vacuum is created by the biased imagination of the subject.

There is no absolute formula for happiness – each unique

condition of life can serve as the foundation for happiness, in its own unique way. You can be happy when married with children, or when married without children. You can be happy when you are single, without a college degree, or with one. You can be happy when you are slim, you can be happy when you are overweight. You can be happy when living in a warm climate as in California, you can be happy when living in Montana, where you have severe winter conditions. As a sumo wrestler, you can be happy when you make it to *yokozuna*, or you can be happy while remaining one of the underdogs all your career, doing small chores, never giving up.

In a nutshell, in order to be happy, you need to accept yourself. Accepting yourself is one of the most important and yet difficult tasks we face in our lives. Indeed, accepting oneself is one of the easiest, simplest and most rewarding thing you could do for yourself – a low-budget, maintenance-free formula for being happy.

The epiphany here is that, paradoxically, accepting oneself as one is often involves **releasing yourself**, especially when there is an illusory self, which you hold to be desirable. You need to let go of the illusory self, in order to accept yourself and be happy.

In Maurice Maeterlinck's play The *Blue Bird*, a girl named Mytyl and her brother Tyltyl go on a trip to find happiness. They think the Blue Bird of Happiness will be found in other places. Despite their efforts, they cannot find the Blue Bird anywhere. Disappointed, they return to their home. They are surprised to find the Blue Bird of Happiness right in their house, tweeting briskly. In fact, the Blue Bird was in their home, all along. What does that tell you?

In 1996, researchers in Italy reported a major discovery in neuroscience. While examining a monkey's brain, they accidentally discovered that its neurons became active when the monkey was doing something. The same set of neurons also became active when the monkey observed others do the same action. Neurons with such properties were consequently named 'mirror neurons'.

Mirror neurons have been discovered in human brains, too. Today, it is thought these neurons are involved in various aspects of communication, including mind reading, where we make estimations of other people's minds. Mirror neurons are considered to be essential when we make comparisons between ourselves and others, a step considered necessary in order to realize what kind of people we ourselves are.

The mirrors in your bathroom reflect your physical appearance. In order to appreciate your own personality, however, you need to have those of others to reflect yourself. Only through realizing the similarities and differences between yourself and others, can you come to a realistic appraisal of your character.

The same was true for Mytyl and Tyltyl. Only after travelling in the wide world, and comparing others with themselves, did they come to realize the actual nature of themselves. Only then could they accept themselves as they truly were. The fable of the Blue Bird of Happiness tells us that we can find our happiness within the unique condition of each of us. The grass might look greener on the other side, but that is only an illusion.

People who come to the *Comiket* and interact with each other on an equal footing know just that. They come to the *Comiket*, in search of the Blue Bird of Happiness. And they find what they are looking for, nowhere else but in themselves. After enjoying being a fantastic anime character in cosplay, they remove their joyous outfits and come back to their own selves.

CHAPTER 10

Accept yourself
for who you are

Tomizo Yamaguchi is the current owner and master of the famous Japanese sweets maker Suetomi. Suetomi has been producing sweets for tea ceremonies and other occasions since 1893.

According to Yamaguchi, sweets representing flowers, for example, are made each with slightly different shapes and colours. It is not that the skills of the craftsmen are faulty so that they cannot reproduce the same result. In fact, the craftsmen deliberately make the shapes different, one by one, because no two flowers in nature are exactly the same.

The most fundamental assumption of modern industry is that artifacts need to be made with as constant qualities as possible. When you make an automobile, for example, the mechanical and electronic parts produced in thousands need to be copies of identical properties. Otherwise, precision manufacturing of automobiles would not be possible.

This kind of approach would not do for creatures of nature, including humans. As we know when we look around us, every person is different. Even identical twins develop different personalities. People tend to perceive individuals belonging to an ethnic group as being homogeneous in character. However, if you look properly, you start to discern the individual differences.

As Yamaguchi aptly observed, variation is one of the greatest hallmarks of nature. To make every sweet slightly different from the other is actually very realistic. Because of the significant roles played by cultural influences and learning, humans certainly exhibit even greater variation than flowers, leaves or other living entities in nature. It is no good trying to be like others, even if there is peer pressure. So there is every reason to relax, and just be oneself.

The Japanese proverb *junin toiro* ('ten different colours for ten different people') expresses the view that there are great variations in personality, sensitivity and value systems among people. In pursuing your *ikigai*, you can be yourself, as much as you like. It is only natural you should be yourself, because each one of us has slightly different colours.

The appreciation of diversity seems to go against the conventional wisdom that Japan is a more or less culturally or ethnically homogeneous country. Its government applies notoriously stringent restrictions on immigration. The sight of salarymen packed in a commuter train, with the station clerks trying to push the herd into the carriages, certainly seems to be a far cry from the idea of respect for individuality. In Japan, there is still a stereotyped image of marriage and family life, and the Japanese government has been slow in adapting legislation treating all kinds of genders and sexual minorities equally.

It is certainly true that the Japanese tend to think that theirs is a unified nation. With globalization, the mindset of the nation is changing, but the Japanese tend to think that they are a homogeneous people. Having said that, there is an interesting depth to the expression of individuality in

Japanese society. The Japanese have a series of small tricks for keeping individuality alive, while striking a harmonious relationship with others.

There are some historical reasons for this. In the Edo era which began in 1603, prior to the modernization of Japan with the Meiji Restoration in 1867, the Tokugawa Shogunate issued a series of executive orders to maintain stability in society, as perceived appropriate in those times. One of the issues often raised was the avoidance of luxury. As the Edo economy grew, some merchants made a lot of money and became huge spenders. Such exhibition of accumulated luxury was considered to have a corrosive effect on social stability, caused by the widening asymmetry between classes. The Shogunate thus issued a series of executive orders prohibiting excessive spending. The rich merchants complied, on the surface, since there was no arguing with the Shogun in those days. However, they did manage to keep their enjoyments secretly. One of the techniques was to use costly clothing materials on the inside of their attire, while outwardly keeping a subdued appearance. The idea of keeping a low outward profile and making inner individuality flourish is wisdom that the people of Japan have nurtured over the years. This technique could be used in any society, especially when social scrutiny is a problem. (Just think of the pressure from social media nowadays!)

The Japanese way of maintaining individual uniqueness whilst maintaining subdued outside appearances is a mixed bag in the modern context. For example, it has made disruptive innovations difficult to nurture and develop in the country, since a disobedient personality such as Steve Jobs or Mark Zuckerberg is not easily tolerated. New forms of services which clash with established businesses, such as Uber or Airbnb, are very slow to take hold in Japan. The inhibition of the expression of individual uniqueness has stifled Japan's educational system, which tends to stress conformity rather than diversity among individuals.

Most Japanese choose to pursue the *ikigai* of individuality in the private domain, probably as the result of the social climate. This hidden approach to the expression of individuality is not the only solution. However, we can at least say it is an interesting one.

To a casual observer, a salaryman might appear faceless. Inside his uninteresting jacket, however, he might be hiding a passion for anime or manga. On week days he might be an obedient clerk in a company. At night and weekends, he might be a star in a *comiket* or a lead singer in an amateur rock band.

There is liberation in the idea that a seemingly conformist person could nurture deep layers of individual personality, which may not be apparent on the surface. In addition, the approach each individual adopts towards his or her life might be actually quite unique. Individual uniqueness is something to be discovered and worked on, not merely assumed and preserved.

Defining the *ikigai* of being an individual in harmony with society at large would reduce much of the stress of competition and comparison. You don't have to blow your own trumpet to be heard. You can just whisper, sometimes to yourself.

A famous tofu maker based in a Tokyo suburb, Takeru Yamashita is a hidden philosopher. He discusses the diversity in the beans, which becomes the single important source material for tofu, as if he is talking about the individuality of the human soul. 'It is Aristotle rather than Plato,' Yamashita says. He also recites a Shakespeare work, to the total bewilderment of the camera crew. Apparently, a masterpiece of Shakespeare has as much to do with the art of tofu making as does the selection of beans. Yamashita's idiosyncratic manner of explaining his approach to tofu making is something you encounter quite often when meeting somebody with a unique approach to *ikigai*, especially in a country where the expression of individuality does not necessarily take flamboyant forms.

Ikigai and happiness come from the acceptance of the self. Recognition from other people would certainly be a bonus. However, it can also hinder the all-important acceptance of the self if put in a wrong context. As Yamaguchi observes, when referring to the way sweets in Kyoto are made, everything in nature is different. We humans are also different, each one of us.

Celebrate who you are! I had the pleasure of having a chat with British comedians Matt Lucas and David Walliams once when they were on a press tour in Tokyo for the promotion of

Little Britain. During our conversation, Lucas confided that he used to be laughed at at school. Therefore, in an action of creative self-defence, he started to make people laugh, before he was laughed at. Walliams agreed, saying that laughter could be the best form of self-defence.

From a cognitive point of view, laughter is considered an instance of metacognition, supported by the prefrontal areas of the cortex. In metacognition, you look at yourself as if observing from the outside. By doing that, you come to terms with your own defects and shortcomings, and supplement your awareness with fresh insight seen from the outside.

You might be afraid to confront the true image of the self. In such cases, a healthy dose of laughter, supported by a metacognition of the self, would help. If metacognition does not lead to mirth straight away, it is always good to have a realistic picture of oneself, even if it is not a favourable one.

The greatest secret of *ikigai*, ultimately, has to be the acceptance of oneself, no matter what kind of unique features one might happen to be born with. There is no single optimum way to *ikigai*. Each one of us has to seek our own, in the forest of our unique individualities. But don't forget to have a good laugh while seeking yours – today and every day!

CONCLUSION

Find your own *ikigai*

Let us look again at the Five Pillars of ikigai:

Pillar 1:   Starting small

Pillar 2:   Releasing yourself

Pillar 3:   Harmony and sustainability

Pillar 4:   The joy of small things

Pillar 5:   Being in the here and now

Now, having read the book, how do these pillars of *ikigai* appear to you?

- Do you have some insights that would help you sort out the problems in life?
- Are you more inclined now to try things, by small

steps, while not necessarily seeking immediate external rewards?

- Would you now see the crucial link between harmony and sustainability?
- Do you feel you would be more relaxed about the particularities that make you, while being more tolerant towards the idiosyncracies of other people?
- Are you more likely now to be able to find pleasure in small things?

It is hoped that this introduction to *ikigai* will allow you to appreciate the significance of these pillars with a renewed and deepened sense of significance. That it will provide you with the insight you need to sort out your specific issues.

The concept of *ikigai* is Japanese in origin. However, *ikigai* has implications far beyond national borders. It is not the case that the Japanese culture is anything special in this regard. It is only that the particular cultural conditions and traditions in Japan have led to the nurturing of the concept of *ikigai*. Indeed, it is quite possible that among the thousands of different languages spoken in the world, there are some concepts similar to that of *ikigai*. Every language is, after all, on an equal footing in that it is the result of the strenuous efforts of its speakers to live and let live, over generations.

Hideo Kobayashi, a respected literary critic in modern Japan, once said that he wanted to live as long as possible. He believed, from his own experience, that another day in life would bring yet another discovery and more wisdom. According to his former editor Masanobu Ikeda, Kobayashi often talked about the 'universal motor', when he looked for a metaphor to describe what is important in life. In every yacht, there is a universal motor, according to Kobayashi. The universal motor does not have much power, but is steady and reliable; in the event of an emergency or adversity, the universal motor will take the yacht safely back to harbour.

Ikigai is like Kobayashi's universal motor. No matter what happens, so long as you have *ikigai*, you can muddle through difficult periods of your life. You can always go back to your safe haven, from where you can start your life's adventures all over again.

As we have seen in this book, *ikigai* does not come from a single value system. It is not written in the orders of God. It comes from the rich resonance of a spectrum of small things, none of which serves a grandiose purpose in life by itself.

The values surrounding *ikigai* that you will have taken on board while reading this book, it is hoped, will inspire you to try new things in your life, and change things step by step. There shouldn't be a loud fanfare to accompany your new beginnings, rather this change in awareness will creep up slowly on you instead of jumping out violently. In life, we need evolution, not revolution. Too often, an illusion towards a revolution in life – where you are swept away by newly found principles, novel ways of thinking and doing, and the idea of starting life all over again – has led people astray.

Because *ikigai* just reinforces your already-held intuitions, the change will be gradual and modest, like life itself.